SEEMS LIKE YESTERDAY

Also by Ann Buchwald
with Marjabelle Stewart

What to Do When and Why, Pre-Teen Manners
Stand Up, Shake Hands, Say How Do You Do
White Gloves and Party Manners

ANN BUCHWALD
INTERRUPTED BY
ART BUCHWALD

G. P. PUTNAM'S SONS
NEW YORK

Published simultaneously in Canada by
Academic Press Canada Limited, Toronto.

Library of Congress Cataloging in Publication Data

Buchwald, Ann.
Seems like yesterday.

1. Buchwald, Art—Biography—Marriage. 2. Buchwald, Art—Homes and haunts—France—Paris. 3. Authors, American—20th century—Biography. 4. Buchwald, Ann. 5. Wives—United States—Biography. I. Buchwald, Art. II. Title.
PS3503.U1828Z6 1980 814'.54 [B] 79-25494
ISBN 0-399-12440-3

Printed in the United States of America

Second Impression

To Joel, Connie and Jennifer Buchwald

SEEMS LIKE YESTERDAY

A Few Words By The Husband

Dear Reader:

The story you are about to read is one woman's version of her thirteen years in Paris from 1949 until 1962. I have a vested interest in how it comes out, since I play one of the main roles in the book—I perform the part of the reluctant suitor and husband who sacrifices a career of fame and fortune in my father's curtain and slipcover business, to marry a poor but honest girl from Warren, Pennsylvania, to make her into one of the most powerful women in Washington today.

Since this is a woman's story, the facts are clouded, distorted, romanticized, and terribly one sided. When I heard my wife was writing about our years in Paris, which to me were the most endearing of my life, I immediately sought legal counsel.

"Does the person you are still married to have the right to reveal confidences and intimate revelations of your years together in the City of Light?" I asked.

The lawyer went behind the counter of the store he was working out of and looked in a book. "Yes," he said, "but since you are still living together you have the right to reply, and can give your side of the story."

I returned home and told my wife that I have been advised by one of the highest-paid lawyers in Washington that since she had decided to tell all about our years in Paris, she had to let me have my say where I felt something she had written might make me look bad in the eyes of all the people who thought I was the perfect husband and father.

"But this is *my* book," she said angrily.

"I am aware of that," I said, "and I will only interrupt where I feel I have been maligned, or when I think you got the facts wrong, or when I believe my contribution will clear the air."

My wife and publisher reluctantly agreed to let me interpose my own comments with the clear understanding that I would not benefit financially or creatively in the product.

The question of who will pay the taxes on my wife's royalties is still to be decided by the courts.

One

The two most important men in my life were Pierre Balmain and Art Buchwald. I met both by accident, and each had a permanent though different effect on my future.

They came into my life in the early fall of 1949, just a few days after my arrival in Paris, the city I had dreamed of for so many years I couldn't believe I was really there. On French soil. In Paris. On the Champs-Élysées. That sunny September afternoon I didn't know what I would end up doing in the months ahead, but I was absolutely certain that I was in the right place, distant though it was from the bridges I had so recently burned behind me. I had come to Paris alone, without a job, but with the firm intention of living there for a full year during which time I would change my life.

I had vowed to find a new career, one that I would not only enjoy but which would allow me to earn an exalted salary of $10,000 a year when I returned to the United States. Ten thousand dollars was the highest figure I dared shoot for since I had spent ten years reaching what seemed an impenetrable ceiling of $7,500.

No one knew the truth about the giant step I had taken. I had lied to my family and all but one of my friends, telling them that I was going to work in a French buying office. Since none of them had ever been to Paris, or knew anything about French buying offices, my lie was swallowed whole.

The day I met Pierre Balmain, I had taken a cab to the Rond-Point, the wide intersection at the bottom of the Champs-Élysées, hoping the famous avenue would boost my failing courage and bring me luck in finding work. How different Paris was from what I'd imagined! The confidence I had felt when I arrived was melting away and I could visualize the other tourists I passed saying, "She certainly isn't a Parisian." I did look 100 percent American. I was short and small, five feet and barely one inch tall and weighed 105 pounds. I wore high-heeled black patent-leather pumps to make me seem taller and the best daytime outfit I could afford, a black-and-white checked suit with a Hattie Carnegie label in it, a strand of five-dollar pearls, white kid gloves, and a handsome leather travel purse. Everything looked and *was* spanking new; I'd bought it all in one afternoon going from floor to floor in Neiman-Marcus the week I quit my job there to come to Paris.

I had short light brown hair which was the curse of my life; it was thin, straight as lampshade fringe, and I could never force it to grow long enough to cover my earlobes. Hairdressers usually ran their hands through it and said, "There's very little I can do with this baby-fine hair of yours." Then they'd give it minimum attention, complaining about it to other clients as they worked. I pincurled it every night of my life, and had done so the night before. But this morning it had behaved worse than usual so I'd slapped on a small straw sailor hat at the last minute. Although the millinery buyer at Neiman-Marcus had assured me it was the newest look for fall, I hated it because it made me look like a prissy high school girl, or like little Ann McGarry dressed up for Sunday Mass. But I did have excellent posture, drilled into my spine by my father, who had served in World War I and who insisted that I "walk like a soldier" even before I was old enough to go to school. Now at twenty-eight, over 3,000 miles away, I finally acknowledged his gift, sure that I looked quite sophisticated and at least five foot three.

I come from a large family of nine girls and two boys. I am the oldest, the first-born daughter, and in many ways the most fortunate: I had my mother's and father's undivided attention for a full sixteen months before anyone else was born. I've always had a hunch I got the best of my mother's dreams, the right if not the duty to live out certain unfulfilled plans she put aside when she became a parent. My mother was strong, self-assured, bright and extremely capable. She was a college graduate who had studied Greek and Latin; she played the piano, organ and cello. More important for her children she talked and acted as though we could accomplish whatever we set out to do; nothing was impossible, God would provide.

My father had quit school at twelve to learn a trade; he became an expert barber. His Irish personality endeared him to hundreds of townspeople who remained his customers for years. At one point he owned a fine barber and beauty shop and bought us a handsome red brick house in the residential part of town. My mother's ambitions for us slipped up another octave.

Then the stock market crashed and totalled big families like ours. By the end of the Depression there were fourteen of us, two parents, eleven children born within sixteen years, and a maternal grandmother whose old homestead we were forced to move into. My father's spirits never rose again.

I wasn't sure how to start out on my mother's uncharted plans for the future she'd envisioned for me. I only sensed that I would never find it in Warren; I knew every inch of the town and had never seen anything that matched the look in my mother's eyes. Evidently I'd have to go somewhere else. I began saying silent goodbyes to apple trees and old stone fences and picnic grounds during high school even though I knew there wasn't a prayer of going off to college. I went to work in Warren and one morning, shortly after I'd received a letter accepting me for a job in the advertising department of a big

Memphis department store, I climbed onto a Greyhound bus and left.

For the past ten years I had worked in department stores starting as a salesgirl in the only "big store" in Warren, Pennsylvania, the town where I was born and grew up. Warren was, and still is, a small community of 15,000 people nestled in the Allegheny mountains in the northwest corner of Pennsylvania. From that little town, where I sold lingerie and infants' wear, I had worked my way out of Warren and into advertising, beginning as a copywriter for basement merchandise at Lowenstein's in Memphis and then moving to Pittsburgh to write accessories ads for Kaufman's. After that I applied for—and to my amazement got—a job as assistant advertising manager for an old, family-owned store called Steinbach's in Asbury Park, New Jersey. The next step was a big one: New York City, where I worked for three years in the buying office of the Associated Merchandising Corporation. I was one of three editors who wrote a weekly fashion bulletin for its fifty affiliated stores. I had traveled fast, but I was always aware that the labor shortage caused by World War II was to a large part responsible for my rapid rise.

In early 1948 the owner of a New York executive placement agency called me at the AMC fashion office and asked if I'd be interested in an interview with Stanley Marcus of Neiman-Marcus in Dallas. He was in town scouting for a fashion director. I gulped. Neiman-Marcus had the finest fashion reputation of any store in the United States; I figured I didn't have a chance. Nevertheless, at the end of that dreary day I sloshed across town in the rain to meet Stanley. I was the last person on his list for an interview. After only ten minutes, he said, "Okay, let's give it a try—see you in Dallas in two weeks." I was ecstatic but sure he'd said yes only because he was bored interviewing.

It was the best job I ever had, and because it was *the* most competitive store in the country, I worked seven days a week, twelve hours a day, and two hours every night in my apartment to keep up with it.

Many years later when Stanley, who had become a close friend, was visiting Art and me in Paris, he teased me about that first meeting. "If you could have seen yourself that day, dripping wet hair, ankle-strap shoes with pieces of slush stuck to your heels, your mascara smudged. . . ."

Ho, ho, ho yourself, I thought. I was right. You were just too tired that February day to look any further.

A Northerner, used to mountains, trees, and crisp clean air, I nearly suffocated in the Texas heat and was bewildered by the lazy drawling speech. Even more depressing was the fact that just as I got used to the way Texans talked, I realized that instead of dating dashing six-foot ranchers I was going out with men shorter than I was; one a dainty, five-foot pediatrician who tackled me at every turn and insisted that a woman's place was in the home.

Now, ten years after starting out I had gambled and come to Paris. If I survived the year I could win a big job back in the States by offering the one thing most merchandise people could not: Paris experience.

Until then, I would have to live poor. My financial assets totalled $1,000 in traveler's checks, a letter of introduction to Pierre Balmain from Stanley Marcus, and the return half of a New York–Paris round-trip airplane ticket, redeemable within one year of purchase. For the moment my main problem seemed to be finding my way around a strange city with a sense of direction so poor that friends often marveled that I hadn't exited my mother's body via her left ear.

In my purse I had a map of Paris, an unwieldy forty-eight-inch-square of paper showing all streets, boulevards, and districts. I had studied it for an hour at the Café de la Paix that morning, marking x's where I lived, where I was sitting at the moment, where I might find familiar-sounding streets. But already I had forgotten the circuitous route that taxi driver had taken from the place de l'Opéra.

I had no idea how to get back to the tiny bedroom I had rented from a French woman and her daughter. Madame Boyer, my landlady, had accepted me sight unseen. I'd written to her at the suggestion of a young Neiman-Marcus fashion artist whose family had known the Boyers years before. My letter to her had closed, "Since I have never been in Paris before, or for that matter anywhere out of the United States, I hope your apartment is centrally located so I'll be able to find my way around."

She had written back, "Do not worry. We live in one of the oldest and best-known areas of Paris." It was true—she lived in the Bastille area where the French Revolution had started, and where poor Marie Antoinette had sat in a dungeon waiting to be decapitated. The apartment was in a 200-year-old building on boulevard Magenta at the place de la République, a seedy, working-class district where most of the French Communists lived. Every building bore an angry-looking poster or a red-splashed slogan vilifying capitalism.

The place de la République was also a major produce center. Every night, just before dawn, farmers from the surrounding countryside trundled into town with truckloads of fresh vegetables which they sold at a noisy open market. As late as 9:00 A.M. the streets were still littered with lettuce and cabbage leaves, the gutter clogged with cut-off stems of carrots, onions, and leeks.

The thought of that morning's slithering streets made me shiver. I hastily turned my attention to the glorious boulevard in front of me. The Champs-Élysées was wide as an interstate highway, filled with six lanes of honking cars, most of them old, black, and dented. The sidewalks were jammed with people hurrying to lunch, impolitely bumping each other and occasionally jostling a slow walker off the curb into the street. The gendarmes directing traffic seemed to be yelling death sentences. How different it was from what I'd imagined. Born into an Irish-Catholic family and educated for years by nuns, I had pictured France as a country dedicated to Catholicism, the Virgin Mary, and a thousand saints. Paris wasn't like that at all! It was the biggest, loudest, wildest city I'd ever seen.

I looked at my watch and saw it was 12:30 P.M. I had been standing around for too long; familiar fears were beginning to rumble inside my rib cage. I'd long ago learned they eased when I began to move, so when the light flashed green I followed the crowd across the boulevard.

Two minutes later I found myself on an elegant street lined with tiny perfume shops, hairdressing salons, and lingerie stores. Then I was in front of an imposing doorway framed with the name PIERRE BALMAIN. "Balmain! Balmain! The one person I know!" I almost shouted. "At least Stanley does or he wouldn't have written that letter of introduction." But my spirits sank as I remembered that the letter was back in my room. If I go back for it, I thought, I'll never find this place again. So I squared my shoulders, lifted my chin, and walked inside.

At the entrance was a small accessories boutique, carpeted in deep red and decorated with small crystal chandeliers. But all the lights were out and the only person I saw was an old man vacuuming the floor. I couldn't have known at that time that all French businesses close from 12:30 to 2:30 P.M. to allow everyone to go home for lunch. I walked over to tbe cleaning man and raising my voice said, "Mister Balmain, s'il vous plaît." I had started using the few French words I'd picked up, but I didn't understand a syllable of the long sentence he mumbled in response. We both shrugged and he pointed his vacuum hose toward a flight of steps. I nodded in thanks, walked up to a small landing, peeked around the remaining half-flight that curved to a floor above, and saw that it too was empty. Then I spotted a beautiful girl, obviously a model, sitting on a windowsill sunning herself.

"Where is Mr. Balmain's office, please?" I asked in English. Staring curiously, she led me through a series of dusky back corridors and up another flight of worn stairs to the open door of an office so imposing I half expected to see a crowned head behind the desk. Instead, there was Pierre Balmain, sandy-haired, tanned, and as far as I could tell, handsome—his face was buried in his hands.

Less than an hour before, Balmain had fired his publicity director. Balmain had long been aware that she kept a bottle of "vin ordinaire" in her desk drawer, but this particular morning she had uncorked it earlier and oftener than usual. At noon as she stood at the top of the stairs waiting to greet a socially prominent client, she had lost her precarious balance and fallen headlong on top of her customer who immediately passed out.

As Balmain slowly raised his head, I said in one breath, "I'm - Ann - McGarry - from - Neiman - Marcus - and - I - have - a - letter - to - you - from - Stanley - Marcus."

Someone later told me that Balmain had never before lunched at his desk, and as long as I worked for him I rarely found him in his office a minute later than 12:15. He ate promptly at 12:30 at his mother's house every day he was in Paris.

Pierre offered me the job out of desperation. My qualifications were inadequate; I spoke no French, I had never done public relations in my life, but I did have one thing to offer. "Do you know the girls at *Vogue* and *Harper's Bazaar*?" he asked. I said I knew them well. He fell silent and once again buried his head in his hands. Then with a mischievous smile he got up and clapped his hands. "Why not?" he said. "We are trying to reach the American press, we are trying to sell to American buyers, yet no one in the entire Couture except me has bothered to learn English. You will talk to them in their own language—would you like to start tomorrow?"

Like Pierre, I met Art Buchwald my first month in Paris, and also by accident; it was in the hotel room of the girl he was dating. At the time, I didn't dream I would ever see him again. In fact, we made such slight impressions on each other that when we met weeks later neither of us could remember the other's full name.

Our first encounter embarrassed me so much that I tried to forget it the moment it was over. Kittie Campbell, an editor from the Philadelphia *Bulletin*, had offered to let me use her typewriter while she was away covering a fashion opening. As Kittie took me up the elevator of the Hôtel Plaza Athenée, she said, "Oh, by the way, there's a friend waiting for me in my room. He's going to help me change my dollars on the black market when I get back."

As we walked into her room, richly furnished with deep-green velvet draperies, an ornately carved bed fit for a princess, and a Louis-something desk, I immediately spotted the man snoozing in a wing chair across the room. He wore a sporty brown hat which was pulled down over his horn-rimmed glasses, and his shirt looked rumpled as if he'd been dozing in that chair for days. He had slipped his feet halfway out of his loafers and made no attempt to stand up when Kittie woke him, saying, "Ann, this is Art Buchwald of the Paris *Herald Tribune.*" Nor did he offer to shake hands. He merely pushed up the brim of his hat, looked at me, and said 'Hi.' "

ART: **My recollection of this first meeting is much different. I thought I was quite polite, but I did not consider meeting another American girl in Paris a very big deal.**

I had been in France for about a year and a half. Briefly the story of how I got there was that I had served in the U.S. Marines during World War II and then went to the University of Southern California on the GI Bill for three years. I was born and raised in New York, and the citizens of that great state had voted to give anyone who had served in the war a bonus of $250. When the check arrived I asked my friends on the *Daily Trojan* where I worked what I should do with the money. Someone suggested I could go to Paris on the GI Bill of Rights. I think he said, "I hear the streets are paved with mattresses."

This seemed like a great idea so I hitchhiked to New York in the spring of 1948 and bought a one-way ticket to Paris on a ship called the *Marine Jumper*, which it did. I arrived in Paris with $100 in my pocket, a huge box of chocolate bars, soap and toilet paper that my sisters had given me because they were certain Paris was on its last legs.

I immediately enrolled in a French language school

called the Alliance Française on the boulevard Raspail, so I would qualify for the GI Bill which paid a living allowance of $75 a month. I also discovered that because I was an American and had dollars I was entitled to gas ration stamps which I could sell to taxi drivers for $25 a month.

In 1948 a student could live like a prince on $100 a month, and from the moment I landed in France I never had any financial problems. There were 60-cent dinners with wine, garrets for $5 a week, and public baths where you could get a hot tub, towel, a sliver of soap, and 15 minutes to soak your body.

I also had a student card which gave me discounts on everything from the Paris Métro to the Paris Opéra.

In the course of my student days in Montparnasse I met a man named Maxime De Beix who worked for *Variety*, the show business journal. I became his leg man at $8 a week. Offsetting the low pay was the fact that it gave me entrée to the French theaters and cinemas and also gave me an excuse to talk to visiting American celebrities at cocktail parties at the Ritz, Plaza Athenée, and George V hotels.

I read the European Edition of the *Herald Tribune* every day and realized they did not have a nightclub columnist. In January of 1949 I went to see the managing editor, Eric Hawkins, and tried to convince him to let me write one. He threw me out. A few weeks later I heard Hawkins had gone back to the United States on home leave, so I returned to the *Trib* offices and asked to see the editor, Geoffrey Parsons, Jr. I said, "The managing editor and I have been talking about me doing a nightclub column." Parsons thought it was a good idea and might produce some advertising. So he hired me to write one for $25 a week, providing I also reviewed films.

When Hawkins came back I was sitting at a desk typing away. It took him a few weeks to get over it and we then became great friends.

I circulated all over Paris and that is how I met Kittie Campbell. She came over to cover the fashion openings and I ran into her at one of them, invited her to dinner, and so on and so on. Whenever I got tired and she was in town I went up to her room to snooze in her chair, where Ann found me that day.

I'm certain that if I had any inkling that someday we would be married I would have stood up when she walked into the room. But how the hell was I to know then that she was going to mean more to me than just another tourist looking for a typewriter?

There is one more point of contention in the story as she tells it and we've been arguing about it for twenty-six years. I insist that her purpose in coming up to the room that day was to ask my help in exchanging her dollars for francs on the black market. (I had a connection named Max.) She insists I never changed any money for her and that she would never have anything to do with a black market. The reason Ann gets so angry about this is that when people ask how we met I always reply, "We both had the same black-market money changer," which I consider the most romantic way you can meet someone in Paris. It certainly is a better line than "through a friend from Philadelphia."

The day I left Dallas, the feature editor of the *Evening News* had offered me $25 to write a series on my first impressions of Paris; so as Kittie scampered off to her next appointment, I walked over to her typewriter, sat down, inserted a clean page of copy paper, and found my mind suddenly blank except for the image of the man slumped in the chair behind me. There wasn't a sound in the heavily carpeted room. I typed "Now is the time . . ." and my name and address over and over, fast at first, then more slowly, until I'd covered a full page. I paused several times to look at notes I'd taken from my purse, and to listen; I prayed that the stranger had gone back to sleep. No sound of snoring. So I typed a second page of nonsense, becoming increasingly nervous because I had never tried to write a straight newspaper story and didn't know how to begin. Finally, a drowsy voice said from the chair:

"What are you trying to do, anyway?"

My God, I thought. Could he have seen what I had written? I gave up, yanked out the page, folded it carefully with the first one, grabbed my notes, and stood up pertly as if I'd done in record time exactly what I'd come to do. "Oh, I was just writing an article about my first days in Paris—I'm here looking for a job," I said. And I fled.

Less than thirty-six hours later, I met Art again. I was eating scrambled eggs, sausages, and toast at unbelievably high prices in the Grill Room of the same Hôtel Plaza Athenée. My French grammar book was propped up against a small carafe of wine and I was studying Lesson II from my nightly Berlitz course. I was trying to concentrate on verb forms so I wouldn't worry over my foolish behavior, eating in one of the most expensive hotels in town, where only Americans on expense accounts could afford the simple home-style food.

From behind me came a voice I immediately recognized: "If you keep eating in places like this, your money won't hold out—mind if I sit down? Kittie is always late." I glared up at him with pure hate. He had once again hit a sore spot. My money was going fast and my spirit was low. "No!" I said sternly. "I have to study." I poked my nose back into my book. "Okay," Art said without disappointment as he sauntered toward another table. Where did he get this uncanny knack of knowing exactly what was scaring me most?

I watched Art leave the restaurant a few minutes later, and only then admitted that it had been my utter loneliness, my longing to hear English spoken, that had led me from my rented room on the other side of the city to this one spot where I knew I could see and listen to Americans.

ART: **I remember the incident, but I was not disturbed by the rejection. I figured anyone studying French grammar at the Relais in the Plaza Athenée couldn't be much fun.**

The next time I saw Art was on a Saturday night in late October when I was dashing toward the Métro on the Champs-Élysées about 9:30 P.M., trying to get home before 10:00, when the concierge would lock the outer door of my apartment building. I had been to the only movie I could find with English subtitles. Suddenly I heard someone shout, "Hey there, McGarry!" I stopped in my tracks, turned and saw Art standing by a café table with a long white napkin flowing from his shirt collar.

He walked across the sidewalk and asked, "Where are you going?"

"Home," I said; "the concierge gets drunk on Saturday nights and if I'm not in my room by ten o'clock, I get locked out."

"But it's only nine-thirty," he argued, and then taking me by the elbow, said, "Come on, I'll buy you a hot fudge sundae," and led me over to the table where he'd been sitting.

Here was that man again, but this time smiling, even twinkling as he said, "I remember your last name but not your first."

I laughed. "And I remember your first but have forgotten your last."

Looking at his immaculate dinner jacket and black tie, I was suddenly overwhelmingly pleased to see a familiar face. I'd been so lonely the last month. All the Americans I knew had left Paris for work or school. Art's words with their emphatic New York accent were as compelling as a favorite childhood song.

"What are you doing, going to a movie alone on a Saturday night?"

"Why are you all dressed up?"

"Have you been anywhere at all except to the movies? Have you been to the Left Bank?"

"No, not to the Left Bank, but something better: I've just gotten a job as publicity director at Pierre Balmain."

"That's great; now here is what we'll do: I'm dressed like this because I have to attend the opening of a nightclub at midnight, but it's only nine forty-five so finish your ice cream and I'll take you to a wonderful place called Chez Inez on the Left Bank. I'll still have time to get you home before I go to the première."

When people ask about our first date, Art always says, "Ann was a pickup on the Champs-Élysées."

ART: **Now the story starts to get interesting. It's true I was having a snack at the Café Colisée because the night-club show didn't start until midnight. I was also café-watching, which is everyone's favorite sport in Paris. The Champs-Élysées is a good spot for this activity and when you're alone it gives you a chance either to run into a pal or fantasize that something wonderful is going to happen to you. My favorite fantasy in those days was that a beautiful French actress who spoke excellent English (my French was lousy) would wander by and say, "Izz thee table taken, Monsieur?" I would stand up (sorry about this, Ann) and say, "It is for you." She would tell me her story. Her husband had gone to Morocco, her lover had left for the weekend to be with his family in Lyons, and she didn't know what to do with herself. I would tell her that I would love to take her to Maxim's but unfortunately the bank draft I was expecting at American Express had not arrived.**

"Pouf," she would say. "I will take you to dinner at Maxim's and then we will go to Jimmy's (the Regine's of its day) and then we will go to my villa across from the bois de Boulogne and I will make coffee and an

> ***omelette surprise* and we will watch the sun rise over the Eiffel Tower as soon as I get into something comfortable."**
>
> **You have to admit it's not a bad fantasy when you're young and single in Paris.**
>
> **Well then I suddenly saw McGarry walking by, and since I gambled my French actress would not come that night I got up and invited her to join me.**
>
> **The truth is that after seeing her for the third time curiosity got the better of me and I wondered what the devil she was doing in Paris, and why was she always by herself.**

Although years later he told me he felt sorry for me—an attractive girl going home alone—that night he showed no signs of sympathy. We found a tiny table in the dark, delicious-smelling nightclub where Inez, an American singer, specialized in spareribs, collard greens, grits, and beer. Later she might sing an old American favorite or two, Art promised. Then he settled into the kind of grilling interview that I later learned was his specialty.

"Where are you from? What does your father do? How many brothers and sisters do you have? Where did you go to school? And then what did you do? How much is Balmain paying you a week? Where do you live? My God, that's not even in Paris, how did you land there? Do you have any friends in town?"—until I blew up.

"Every time I meet you, you blast me with questions! You sound like a census-taker; a researcher—no, I've got it—you're a frustrated advertising man. You get all the facts and then write zingy slogans to captivate the masses."

Art started to shout that I had insulted him *and* his writing. "Never!" he yelled at me across the minuscule table as we sat surrounded by lovers. "I hate advertising, everything about it. Sure it's big money, but I've never worried about making money and I never will. I'm a real writer, a newspaperman."

"I KNOW you're a writer; I read the *Herald Tribune*, and you've got a lot of funny ideas, but your grammar is lousy. I found four or five mistakes in your last column. You must think a comma is something you sink into when you're sick."

Oblivious of everyone and everything around us we continued fighting. At 1:00 A.M. Art looked at his watch and said, "Well, I missed the opening, the hell with it, let's go home." We hailed a taxi and rode for miles, Art asking every few minutes if we were anywhere near my room, frightened that he would not have enough to pay the fare. As we pulled up to my apartment building, I sat very still wondering how to apologize for ruining his evening; but as I opened my mouth to speak, Art's arms crept around me, pulling me close to him, and he kissed me with such sweet and surprising fervor that I didn't say a word. I had the single happiest feeling I'd ever experienced and I didn't even notice that for the first time since I'd moved in, the concierge had forgotten to bolt the doors.

ART: **I was making a pass—a simple straightforward pass—and to her it was some sort of commitment. Good grief.**

The next morning, Sunday, the phone woke me at noon and I stumbled groggily toward the dining room where the old-fashioned instrument hung on the wall. It was Art.

"Did I tell you last night that I'm the official Jew in charge of waking up Catholics for Mass? If you hurry you can also get to the markets before they close at one-thirty; buy what you cook best for dinner and I'll bring the wine . . . now GO!" and he hung up. As I obediently dressed I recalled telling Art that my landlady and her daughter were away on a week's vacation.

Promptly at seven that night Art appeared at the door and handed me a bottle of cheap Algerian wine—the first brown wine I'd ever seen.

ART: **All right, I will admit she did intrigue me a little. First I didn't like her telling me off and I wanted to get that**

straightened out. Second, besides my fantasy life I really didn't know that many girls in Paris, and third, I liked her when she got angry. So when I woke up the next morning I decided to give her a call. Also I had filed away that she was spending the weekend in Paris alone and since I had no plans why not have her cook up a dinner for me at her place and see where it led?

There is one libelous thing that has to be corrected at this point and that is that I have NEVER, NEVER in all my life ever brought a girl a bottle of Algerian wine. As food and wine editor of the *Trib* (a title I gave myself while writing about nightclubs), I wouldn't have been able to drink the stuff, much less ask the woman I was dining with to share it. And, from a more practical point of view, if we split a bottle of Algerian wine (I'm talking about 1948 vintages now), we both would probably have gotten sick and the evening would have been a complete waste. The wine I brought that night was a very respectable Beaujolais. It was young, slightly fruity, and had a pleasant bouquet to it. It only shows you how nervous Ann was that night to mistake a French grape for an Algerian bottle of mud.

Once inside, Art headed straight for the antiquated iron stove where I was cooking green beans and new potatoes and trying to grill lamb chops. He lifted the cover of a kettle and said, "Don't you know you're supposed to wash vegetables before you cook them? These beans are filthy." The bell had rung for the next round.

At church I had made a mental grocery list during the French sermon, which I no longer tried to translate; then I had darted from church into a half-dozen small markets for bread, cheese, pastry, fruit, vegetables, and meat. I was handed each purchase in a curled cone of old newspapers since French merchants believed paper bags a frivolous expense. Lacking a shopping bag, I had kept dropping the beans and potatoes so it wasn't any wonder if they were still a little dirty. Back in the apartment I'd spent an hour trying to light the impossibly old-fashioned stove. I'd used up a large box of kitchen matches before I learned the secret of lighting the broiler; and afraid to turn it off, I'd let it burn all afternoon. The kitchen was hot as a sauna, but the heat didn't seem to bother Art, who just took off his jacket.

When dinner was over he said innocently, "Now show me the rest of this apartment," and walked straight through to my bedroom.

"That's a silly bed," he said.

"I think it was originally a love seat. Those high wood sides. . . ."

"I take it back; it's not so silly when you come to think of it."

We squeezed ourselves onto the bed and fell into each other's arms. After a time I had to push aside his hands.

"If you intended to say no, how come you wore a dress that unlaces all the way down front?" he said.

"It's still no . . . and it laces *up*, too."

But I felt terrible when he left.

Over the next weeks, Art and I devised an arrangement which he termed "platonic." He outlined it this way: "I get invitations to all the big openings and receptions because of my column, and since you ought to meet as many new people as possible to get ideas for Balmain, I'll just tell you when something important is coming up and you can say yes or no—it will be perfectly platonic, okay?"

The plan held up well for two glorious months. While we were at one gala event he would tell me about the next. When we attended the opening of Lasserre Restaurant with its electronically controlled ceiling which could be rolled aside to let the moon shine down on diners, he whispered, "Wait until you see the Paris Opera House tomorrow night! Even the French President will be there." When Gordon Heath and Lee Payant, the folk singers, opened one of the first American bars on the Left Bank, Art squeezed my hand under the table, saying, "Edith Piaf is going to make a special appearance Saturday night at Chez Carrère."

We went to concerts, to lavish country homes owned by American film producers, to Maxim's and the Tour d'Argent and the Ritz Bar. Sometimes we took with us American businessmen on their first trips to Paris, presidents of companies, chairmen of boards, all reduced to helplessness when their working hours were over. "Take us to see the *real* Paris," they'd say and we'd stay up all night, starting at Chez L'Ami Louis, our favorite restaurant, visiting quaint little bars, taking them into St.-Eustache, Paris's famous crumbling church where Masses began at 1:00 A.M. for working people who had to be on the job at dawn. Usually we'd end up at Les Halles eating onion soup at a counter crowded with bloody-aproned butchers.

ART: **One of the galas during this time had repercussions on my professional career. It was the opening of *Joan of Arc* at the Paris Opéra. Walter Wanger was proud of the picture, which had been criticized in the U.S. The fact that the French had turned over the Opera House for the première was a feather in his cap. As film critic of the Paris *Herald Tribune* my reviews were of great importance to American producers, directors, and publicity men because they appeared in English, which was the only language they could read.**

I must admit I did a mischievous thing. Instead of reviewing the Wanger picture I wrote a funny story about taking a bribe of two passes for another RKO film from the publicity man in exchange for NOT reviewing the movie.

Wanger was furious and attacked me at an American Club luncheon, saying the reason I didn't review the picture was that I was immature and inadequate.

The reporters wanted to know how I felt about his comment and I replied, "In France when a producer doesn't like what a critic says he challenges him to a duel. If Mr. Wanger will send his seconds we'll discuss weapons."

> **The story made the news service wires and the French press had a ball with it. One headline in *France Soir* proclaimed TWO AMERICANS TO FIGHT FOR THE VIRGIN OF ORLEANS.**
>
> **I was quite pleased with myself, but Ann was furious with the publicity and wanted to know where I came off attacking someone like Walter Wanger. She said I was destroying any chance of making it in the newspaper world and she didn't want to have anything to do with someone who made a spectacle of himself. I told her it was none of her damn business what I did, and if she didn't like it, it was just tough luck.**
>
> **This was just the first of many fights we have had over the years when she thinks I've gone too far. But everyone in the humor business walks a fine line when it comes to how far he can go, and he doesn't like someone else telling him where the line is. In some cases Ann's been right, but as long as I've known her I've never admitted it. In fact, although she never knew it her reaction to the Joan of Arc incident almost made me decide to break off our relationship.**
>
> **I wanted a girl who would have said at that moment "Sock it to him, Baby."**

One week just before Christmas Art called me at Balmain and with great excitement said he had tickets for a very special one-man show Yves Montand was giving that night at the Théâtre des Champs-Élysées.

"You have to go; you can't say no."

I listened, hesitated, and then told a big fat lie. The truth was I had a date that night with Jim Nolan of the Paris *Herald Tribune*. In fact, I had been dating Jim and one or two other men from time to time, but that Friday morning something warned me not to admit to any non-Buchwald social activities.

"I have a terrible stomachache," I said. "And I'm on my way home this minute to spend the day in bed with a hot water bottle."

Art sounded crushed.

That same evening I borrowed a long black dress from Balmain's collection, a Persian lamb jacket from his furrier, pinned a bunch of delicate silk violets on my shoulder, and went out to dinner with Jim. At midnight we walked into Chez Carrère, then the most popular restaurant for nightcaps, and I immediately spotted Art sitting at the bar with Bob Capa and a group of *Life* magazine photographers. I whispered urgently to Jim, "We can't stay here," and pulled him back onto the street; but not before Art had seen me in all my borrowed finery with a friend from his own newspaper.

ART: **Chez Carrère, off the avenue George V, was the favorite hangout in the late '40s and early '50s for a gang of us including Irwin Shaw; John Huston; Anatole Litvak, the director; Peter Viertel, the screenwriter; Bettina, the French model; Bob Capa and Dave Seymour, the photographers; and American entertainers such as Lena Horne who were working or living in Paris. The front part of it was bar where we drank and the main room was a very chi-chi nightclub where Edith Piaf, Yves Montand, Eddie Constantine, and other French singers performed. From my first day in Paris I discovered that no one seemed to go to bed before three or four in the morning whether you were living it up on the Left Bank in some rundown café or swilling champagne in the Right Bank boîte. I'm sure we all slept sometime, but for the life of me I can't remember when.**

The next morning when I left my office at noon—I had gone in on Saturday to quietly type some letters to my family—Art was waiting outside the building. His hands were jammed into his pockets and he seemed determined not to look at me. Instead he kept kicking the side of the building as he muttered angrily, "If there's anything I can't stand it's a liar."

"I'm truly sorry I lied, but you did say we were platonic, so. . . ."

"I guess I don't want us to be platonic anymore, that's all."

It was a turning point. We smiled, blushed, and walked up the street holding hands like little kids who've just decided to be best friends.

A few weeks after he had agreed to stop being platonic, he gave me a beautiful, non-platonic bracelet from Hermès and on Christmas Eve as we ate at Monseigneur while the Russian violinists tried to play "White Christmas" and "Jingle Bells," Art whispered softly, "I've got a swell idea: tell the people you live with that you've been invited to the country next weekend. Take a small suitcase to the office to make it look real, but then come over to my hotel. No one will ever see us; we won't leave my room til Monday."

ART: **It is essential at this moment that I make certain things perfectly clear. I had come to Paris to be a great writer in the tradition of Hemingway, Eliot Paul, and Henry Miller. In order to write the Great American Novel which I was determined to do at this stage of my life, I did not want any romantic complications. I explained this to Ann on our first real date in the bedroom of her Bastille apartment. I used the word "platonic" because I had just read it somewhere in a book. It was a good word and I felt my conscience was clear.**

Paris is a city where foreigners feel they can make all sorts of promises without having to live up to them. For one thing when it comes to romance you have no families looking over your shoulder demanding what your intentions are. If you're dating an American girl you don't have to fear facing an irate father or mother, or

worse still, a brother who wants to know why you're messing around.

A love affair in Paris is a very special thing to be remembered and cherished and even cried over when one or the other parties must return to the United States.

Without going into details my fondest memories of Paris were of the times I took the girl of the moment down to the Gare St.-Lazare after a two- or three-week fling, and kissed her goodbye just before she boarded the boat-train to the ship that would take her home. This scene of the dark cold station, with the steam escaping from the engine of the train and the tearful lovers, has been filmed by almost every movie director who has ever made a film in Paris.

I would even run alongside the train as the girl leaned out the window waving her handkerchief, her face wracked with grief.

When the train finally disappeared I usually went into the coffee shop, ordered a café filtre, wiped the perspiration from my forehead, and said, "Whoo. That was close." On one occasion I actually met an arriving boat-train half an hour later, managing to pull myself together in time to greet a college girlfriend who had crossed the Atlantic on the same boat my other girl was taking home.

This may sound as if I were playing a cruel game, but that's how Americans lived in Paris in those days and when you're young and not interested in marriage there is nothing wrong with this.

In retrospect I realize my big mistake with Ann was getting jealous of Jim Nolan. My ego was hurt and that is why I was waiting outside Pierre Balmain that morning to tell her off. I was so emotionally upset that I

blurted out that nonsense about not wanting to be platonic anymore. I really didn't know what I was getting into, but I certainly did not mean that I wanted to go steady, which is how Ann interpreted this remark. I imagine it was a turning point because I never did take anyone down to a boat-train after that. But at the same time I still did not have any intention of getting involved. How can someone write the Great American Novel if he has to worry about meeting the same girl every night for dinner?

I was tense and painfully self-conscious as Art and I pushed through the squeaky revolving door of his hotel, the Des États-Unis, for our first clandestine weekend. I was wearing the only warm coat I owned, a spectacular red and black reversible cape created by Pierre who designed a special four-part wardrobe for me at the beginning of every season. ("I don't care how much you like those clothes you brought from Neiman-Marcus; I never want to see any of them again. From now on you will wear only Balmain models," he had ordered the week I went to work for him.)

But I had forgotten to reverse the coat to its black side. I was so conspicuously scarlet in that lobby filled with bearded, drably clad Americans that several of them shouted "Hiya, Art!" from the bar the moment we stepped through the door. In shriveling embarrassment I followed Art into the shabbiest elevator on the Left Bank. It was dinky as a cell and had a large, flyspecked sign, handsomely lettered in Polish: "PROSZE ZAMKNAC DRZWI" The message reeked of intrigue but translated into PLEASE CLOSE THE DOOR. The actual words were adopted by the tenants as a secret fraternity greeting.

ART: **It may not have been the elevator of the Prince de Galles, but it did have one advantage over the elevators in most of the swank hotels in Paris and that is it only took its passengers UP. If a lady changed her mind**

when she got to a gentleman's room she had to walk down. It sounds like a small factor, but in many cases it did tip the scales in favor of the person occupying the room.

Art's room was barely eight feet square. Every inch was taken up by his bed, a nightstand with a lamp, one chair, one small closet, and in the corner a small washbasin and a bidet. It was also very dark. Before he could stop me, I pulled back the curtains covering his only window. Had it been open I would have scraped my nose on the brick wall of the building next door. Art said, "I told you it was a friendly, intimate place."

Looking around, stalling for time, I spied a white Jean Dessès couture box under his bed. "What are you doing with that?"

"Oh, that box is fulla stuff I'm storing for my sister," Art said nonchalantly.

I learned later that the box belonged to an airline stewardess.

On the wall by his bed was a house telephone. No one in the hotel could make or receive outside calls except from a pay phone in the lobby. The only bathroom for all the rooms on Art's floor was a half flight down.

I was aware of every nerve in my body, every beat of my heart, as I began undressing, my back turned to Art. Although part of me was sinfully guilty, another part was courageously brave as the day I first dived off a ten-foot board. I giggled as I removed my Balmain dress, my shoes, garter belt, and dark seamed nylons. I wouldn't be doing this anywhere but Paris, I kept thinking. And I rationalized: at least I'll know what to do on a honeymoon if I ever get married. When I turned around, I was relieved to see that Art was already in bed, his arms outstretched, his soft brown eyes filled with love and understanding.

For years afterward, Art insisted that he had been a virgin when we first made love that afternoon. His story is so involved and minutely detailed, starting with sexual near-misses from eleven years old, that it is almost convincing. But that first time it was clear to me that he knew exactly what to do and that I had a lot to learn in a hurry.

We didn't leave the room that night, the next day, or the next night except to tiptoe down the hall to the bathroom or for Art to make daring forays to the hotel snack bar which supplied us with the most delicious breakfasts I'll ever eat: long loaves of warm, freshly baked bread heaped with American PX peanut butter and accompanied by steaming cups of café au lait.

My inhibitions fled. We made love, slept, ate, laughed, and made love again. Between Friday night and Sunday afternoon all my guilty qualms disappeared. I was an ocean away from condemnation. I was free, and I knew it because for the first time in my life I forgot to go to Mass.

We left Art's room late Sunday afternoon to have supper in a bistro before I returned to my boarding house. I dashed from the elevator toward the revolving doors as if my clothes were on fire. But my haste was in vain. Several of Art's friends waved and called "A bientôt" and "Au revoir" as we fled.

ART: **Ann's description of the Hôtel des États-Unis is fairly accurate if you were a stranger visiting it for the first time. To me it was a romantic home away from home. It was located in the heart of Montparnasse and had been given to a group of Polish veterans who had fought with the French in World War II. The inhabitants were all nationalities with a preponderance of American GIs.**

My room was located on the third floor and the walls were very thin. This made sleep slightly difficult as all sorts of things were going on at all hours. One of my favorite memories was of a Spanish dancer who lived in the next room and entertained male friends after she finished work at three o'clock in the morning. On one of these occasions I was awakened to hear the bed squeak-

ing loudly through the walls and then "clack, clack, clack," more bed squeaking, some moaning and groaning, and then "clack, clack, clack." Finally I heard a gruff male voice shout "For Christ's sake. Put down those Goddamn castanets."

The hotel had a bar where many expatriates hung out. It also was located around the corner from Reid Hall, an American college dorm, where young coeds stayed while they were spending their Junior Year Abroad. I'm proud to say many of them received the best part of their education at the Hôtel des États-Unis.

In the daytime the bar was rather quiet while everyone nursed their hangovers. But at night, life began. Love affairs were started or ended, there were occasional fights between the Poles and the French over who won the war, and arguments over Jean-Paul Sartre, Camus, and Proust. It was a time when everyone claimed they were either writing a book, painting a great work of art, or thinking about enlisting in the Foreign Legion.

None of us ever talked about "finding ourselves." Most of us either knew, or pretended to know who we were. In order for the ex-GIs to collect their subsistence checks we had to prove we were going to school. Those of us who were attending the Alliance Française resolved this matter by giving the lady who took attendance 1000 francs a month (about $2.25) to mark us present.

We went to museums, made occasional forays to St.-Germain-des-Prés, took walks along the Seine, and offered ourselves as guides to the more affluent tourists.

The Hôtel des États-Unis became world famous when one of its boarders, Gary Davis, an ex-U.S. bomber pilot, decided to go down to the United Nations, then meeting in Paris, and give up his American passport to become a "Citizen of the World." The idea of an American giving up his passport in 1948 was mind-boggling and Gary overnight became a media hero.

Our bar was besieged with reporters and cameramen from all over the globe. We were interviewed by American, British, French, and German papers as well as by correspondents from behind the Iron Curtain. Intelligence agents from various countries showed up as did many young people who wanted to join Gary's movement.

Even the Ford Foundation sent someone over to see if they were interested in financing Gary.

This invasion of privacy was not welcomed by the rest of the tenants. For one thing Gary announced he wanted to make the hotel the World Headquarters of his Citizen movement. The Poles became very excited and we found eviction notices in all our mailboxes saying we had to get out in two weeks. We refused, and when the first month went by and Gary had problems paying his rent the Poles asked us to stay and Gary to leave.

Another thing took place about that time (the reader will have to forgive me if I get these periods mixed up since everything was happening so fast). Truman had proclaimed the Marshall Plan to save Europe from going Communist. The idea was to give billions of dollars to our allies to help them rebuild their industries. America would show Europe the way, not only with powerful injections of financial aid, but good old American know-how. Headquarters for the Marshall Plan were set up at the Hôtel Talleyrand and Averell Harriman was sent over to get things moving.

Since the United States was short of Americans abroad to administer the plan, anyone who happened to be in Paris at the time could get a job with the program.

Several disreputable types from the Hôtel des États-Unis went down and applied for positions as guards or in the mail room. In a few months these same people were sitting behind desks in charge of the coal and steel industry for the Benelux Countries, or telling the Dutch how to make cheese.

The irony of all this is that we rebuilt Europe so well that they've been clobbering us in trade ever since.

As soon as my pals went on the Marshall Plan payroll they found classy apartments in Paris and moved out of the Hôtel des États-Unis. But they were replaced by other ex-GIs and we never lacked for drinking companions or playmates.

This then was the place I brought Ann for our first illicit weekend. She was much more sensitive about what others in the hotel were thinking than was necessary. No one to my knowledge ever paid any attention to who was going upstairs and who was going downstairs, as long as they didn't stay in the bathroom too long.

I have one short comment on the virginity story I told Ann. It was a good story and even if she didn't believe it, she wanted to believe it, which to me is the same thing. I've stuck with it for twenty-seven years and I'll be damned if I'm going to change it now.

Following that weekend in Art's hotel, we established a new pattern which was slightly unclear to me except for one fact: Art would remain the free spirit he had always been. Although we would not date other people, we would not take each other seriously, either.

We knew that we had no future together and that marriage was out of the question. Catholic daughters don't marry Jewish sons, and vice versa.

We continued to eat in a different restaurant almost every night so Art could do reviews for "Paris After Dark." He always paid for my dinner so the restaurant owner couldn't later complain to the *Herald Tribune* if he wrote a bad review.

One night he told me that we were going to the Tour d'Argent, invited by a couple whom I would love. As Art led me to a table overlooking the Seine I saw that we were dining with Lauren Bacall and Humphrey Bogart. As we sat down Bogey lifted his martini glass toward his wife and said in mock anger, "Happy Birthday, my ass—d'you realize that tonight I have to celebrate because my wife is now exactly one half my age?" It was Betty's twenty-sixth birthday. Later we became good friends and Betty more than anyone else was responsible for my staying in Paris with Art.

On nights when there were no new restaurants to check out, we ate at Chez Henriette's, in an old building on the Left Bank, where we could stuff ourselves on veal patties with cream sauce, mashed potatoes, fresh French bread and butter, salad, dessert, and coffee—all for 95¢ a person.

In my weekly letters home, I reported everything to my mother except my true relationship with Art. During our first year together Art and I were inseparable. Even when Art traveled, it never occurred to me to date another man. When he was out of town, I worked extra long hours at Balmain, did my laundry, got frizzy $5 permanents, caught up on my voluminous family correspondence, and waited for his return. Art wrote daily from wherever the *Trib* allowed him to wander, his letters often arriving a week after he'd gotten back to Paris.

In later years, to save face with our children, we said we had lived together, but we never actually did so.

Early in the year I did leave the family with whom I'd been boarding. I moved out not only because of their anti-Semitic hatred of Art, but also because their cleaning lady confronted me one Monday morning with a bed sheet from the laundry basket. Red-faced, she shook it at me triumphantly. "Mademoiselle, there was a man in your bed last night! I have found more than wrinkles on your sheets and it will be my duty to report this atrocity to Madame when she comes back from vacation."

Shamed into helplessness, I called Art and wept the story into the phone. He told me to pack at once and wait for him to call back. Within an hour, he had located a room for me to rent in the apartment of a Countess de Bon Répos on avenue Madrid, a few short blocks down from the Arch of Triumph and only one Métro stop from Balmain's corner.

There were several Americans living there and I might have stayed longer if the countess hadn't been stone deaf. She lived in fear of intruders, so whenever she felt like going to sleep, sometimes as early as 10:00 P.M., she carefully turned three massive bolts on her front door and locked me out. She had given me a key for only the master lock. The next morning she was always remorseful. "I thought you were home," she would mutter dizzily. Each time it happened Art and I would pound on the door and scream into the keyhole, but we never once aroused her. Therefore at least once a week I would be forced to check into a hotel on the rue Pierre-Charron where Art knew the night desk clerk. Art would pay for my room in advance and kiss me goodnight as I stood by the elevator dressed in a long evening dress and carrying only a dainty evening purse, no toothbrush, no suitcase. At dawn the next morning, I would have to creep out of the hotel, hail a taxi to the countess's apartment, shuck off my evening clothes, and dress for work.

ART: **This is a good story and I'll let Ann stick with it since it's her book. But I doubt if I would check Ann into a nice hotel on the Pierre-Charron and leave her there alone all night. I'm not that kind of a cad.**

Living with the countess was not only expensive and embarrassing, but every bath was a miserable ordeal. Like all Paris apartments and houses, hers was so minimally heated that the bathroom was as cold as a morgue, its tiled floor a frozen slab. On awakening my first morning, I was surprised to find her waiting for me in the hall as I stumbled sleepily from my bedroom. She handed me a dented old teakettle full of boiling water. Like a robot I took it without question and put it on the bathroom floor while I turned on the faucets in the tub. Ice water gushed from both taps. I tried the small washbasin mounted unusually high on one wall—again, water so cold it hurt my fingers. I lunged for the teakettle and from that morning on used the tiny washbasin to sponge-bathe one part of my body at a time, rationing the hot water in the kettle down to the last tepid rinse into which I'd hoist first one foot, then the other.

ART: **Ann may have been contemptuous of the Hôtel des États-Unis but we always did have hot water—at least I think we did. In any case I'll take a full brigade of Polish war veterans to one French landlady any day of the week.**

In early March of 1950, seven months after I'd arrived in Paris, I was still living my Spartan life at the countess's apartment, but Art had lucked into a sunny studio room on the top floor of an old residential building at 24 rue du Boccador, a quiet street around the corner from the Hôtel George V. Though Art said goodbye to his beloved Hôtel des États-Unis with some reluctance, I was relieved when he moved out. I would no longer have to sneak past his friends in the lobby.

Two weeks after he moved to his aerie on the rue du Boccador he announced with a sexy gleam in his eyes that the room next to his was being vacated and that I could have it if I wanted it. The rent was $32 a month. Art's room, being larger, was $45 a month. He had space to spare, a big desk in the corner, a fireplace, and double armoire closet. My room was half the size, but I loved it.

The cleaning woman who lived in a servant's room at the end of the hall agreed for a small monthly tip to wake us each morning with huge cups of steaming hot coffee, a luxury I enjoyed as long as we were there.

When I first moved in, I didn't realize how many other Americans already lived in the handsome old five-story apartment building.

Irwin Shaw had joyfully bidden farewell to the United States that winter, and with his wife Marian and their three-year-old son Adam, moved to Paris. Irwin's novel, *The Young Lions*, had been published the previous year. It was a smash. He was rich, famous, and the one handsome celebrity every hostess in Paris wanted to capture. The Shaws were the most affluent residents in the building. They were great hosts and the most fun to be around.

Their apartment was spacious and furnished with warmth, charm, and Marian's ingenuity. Paintings hung on every wall from the front door to the bathrooms. Vases of anemones brightened tables year-around, and a blazing fireplace glowed continuously on cold days. We all tended to gather there for nightcaps after parties. Marian would produce cheese, crackers, and cold beer while we rehashed the evening or traded news and gossip. No matter how late the hour, little Adam would eventually hear us and amble out of his bedroom dressed in a plaid bathrobe—looking like a diminutive boxer—to listen and watch. Irwin was teaching Adam to play chess. "The earlier they start, the better," he said. By the time Adam was four he had mastered a few key moves and when the doorbell rang he astonished guests by calling out, "How about a game of chess?"

ART: **Getting Ann to move into 24 rue du Boccador was a stroke of genius on my part. It meant I didn't have to take her home after a long night on the town or whatever. It also meant that we could live together, but in separate rooms. And most of all it saved me thousands of francs in taxi bills. Of course if she hadn't moved in we might never have gotten married and then these memoirs of our life in Paris would have been written by**

Ingrid Bergman or Audrey Hepburn or some other lucky woman.

Teddy White and his wife Nancy lived on the floor above the Shaws. They'd moved to Paris when Teddy left Time-Life, Inc., as its Far East correspondent so that he could finish his book *The Mountain Road,* which later won a Pulitzer Prize. Their two children, David and Heyden, were both born while the Whites lived at 24 rue du Boccador. Heyden narrowly missed being born in the building's elevator. Nancy and Teddy were rushing to the American Hospital when they discovered to their horror that the elevator was stuck. There was a simple reason: Art and I were standing talking with its door open on the ground floor. Teddy screamed down the shaft, "Get out of the elevator, Buchwald, and close the Goddamned door quick! Nancy's having a baby up here!" Heyden was born five minutes after the hysterical Whites reached the hospital.

Teddy had the best library in the building, a wall of books. We all borrowed regularly from him, and he kept track of every book removed from his shelves. We had to sign our name, the date, and the book title on a small pad glued to his bookcase, using a pencil attached to a long string he had nailed to the wall. One rainy Sunday afternoon, just as Art and I reached a most delicious stage of lovemaking, there was a tap on my door, followed by Teddy's voice asking softly, "Annie, have you finished *Thunder Over China*? You've had it for eight days and someone else wants it."

On the second floor were Theo and Midge Benahume, the Whites' closest friends. Theo was handsome, daring, and the entrepreneur of the group. He had rounded up every dollar he could borrow, throwing in his own life savings to boot, to invest in a revolutionary product: the ballpoint pen, invented by Milton Reynolds, another American, whose sales pitch was: "It writes under water." All of Theo's friends feared he would lose every nickel he'd put up, but we were wrong. He became a millionaire. One night I actually tried writing with his pen under the water in my bath. It worked, but the words ran off the page.

Theo's wife Midge always looked heavenly and appeared as if she'd just been outfitted by Christian Dior. The rest of us listened intently to all of Midge's fashion discoveries: a dressmaker who would copy a Balenciaga dress for $50, an artisan who made jewelry for the Couture but also sold it wholesale to anyone willing to walk up six flights of rickety stairs to her loft, a shop with unbelievable discounts on the newest French perfumes. One tip from Midge and we rushed out the next day to save money.

On the fifth floor, our floor, but in a secluded wing closed off by french doors, Raoul Levy lived with his wife and infant son in a large sunny apartment. Although they were French, we considered them part of our American group since Raoul was heavily involved with American filmmaking. He was the man who had discovered Brigitte Bardot when she was eighteen years old, and produced her first film, and perhaps had also fallen in love with her. One night Art and I went to dinner at Raoul's country house where Brigitte was the guest of honor; his eyes never left her even when his wife stood nearby. For reasons we could only guess—Raoul's later films lost as much money as his first ones had made—one day he took out his revolver and killed himself. No one could patch together the whole story, because his wife and son disappeared almost immediately.

ART: **Vingt-Quatre rue du Boccador plays a very important part in this story. The housing arrangements were as described. I had a large studio on the fifth floor with a bathroom in the hall. Ann's room was next door, and could either be approached by walking into the hall and knocking on her door—or going out on the balcony and tapping on her window. I much preferred the window particularly in the spring and summertime, as it saved me the trouble of putting on a bathrobe. The balcony, which wound all around the fifth floor to the avenue George V side of the building, offered the ultimate romantic's view of Paris. Also, if one looked up from the street, the person might see an American climbing out**

of one window and into another. On occasions when Ann was mad at me she refused to open the window. Then I would start shouting through it.

I also had begun to put a hat collection together. Every time I went to the Flea Market I bought a special hat. I owned a top hat from the early 1900s, a French Marshall's hat, a Kaiser helmet, and even a Miner's hat with a candle in the part which gave off light. When we had a fight I would put on one of the hats, go over, and start knocking on the window. The combination usually worked. It's very hard for a woman to keep her window closed when there is a man on her balcony in boxer shorts and a miner's cap pleading to get in.

Everyone in the building was our friend, only most were better friends of Ann's than they were of mine. Nobody was fooled by the fact we had two rooms, and pretty soon there was a conspiracy, particularly amongst the wives at 24 rue du Boccador, to legitimize our living arrangements. Marian Shaw, Nancy White, and Midge Benahume all decided I had the best of both worlds and they didn't like it one bit. Even Irwin, Teddy, and Theo were on Ann's side, probably because I was so happy and they envied me.

As time went on Art and I continued to battle out our relationship. Our real problem was that neither of us wanted to admit we loved each other. I yearned to hear Art say, "I love you," but he refused as adamantly as if I'd asked him to change his name. "I have never said those words to anyone, and I don't think I ever will."

I settled for being close to Art, seeing him night after night, at Monseigneur's or at Gordon Heath's Left Bank bar, which was plainer but even more romantic. Art and I would sit close together, trembling with desire and whispering terrible accusations at one another. "You're hopeless!" "You don't understand that I must be FREE, F–R–E–E!" "You are a man of no morals, no principles," "I'm not the marrying kind," "I wouldn't marry you if we were the last people on earth." Usually I started our fights. I was stuffed to my toes with guilt. How could I go on loving, and making love with, a man who vowed never to make a commitment?

After such fights we would taxi home in silence and casually say "G'night." Then, when I was safely in my room, I would collapse on my bed and sob into my pillow until Art made one of his balcony visits, bringing his favorite book, *Best Loved Poems of the American People*, and began reading as if to a packed auditorium, "A poem for forgiveness . . . ," "A poem for understanding . . . ," whichever one he had selected for that particular crisis. He would finish with the author's name, usually "Anonymous." Then he would step into my room, into my arms, into my narrow bed where, when we stopped laughing, we made love until dawn. At first light Art would peek into the hall to be sure it was empty, and then pop back to his own room.

We lived side by side on rue du Boccador for over two years, deliriously happy one week, not speaking to each other the next. Art considered our arrangement ideal, but I worried about the future. I was always there at the end of the day, yet no ties bound him. He could still take off on an hour's notice for any corner of the world, with no more comment than "I'll write every day!"

Still I'll never forget those years and all the fun we had making up after our fights.

Two

If life with Art was opening new horizons, my days at Pierre Balmain were like a series of shock treatments. Nothing jibed with what I'd learned in any previous job. A French Couture house is as different from a department store as a mansion is from a tent. And the year I got my job, Paris fashion was at its peak. Balenciaga and Schiaparelli held sway and several new designers had begun building young and exciting reputations: Christian Dior, Jacques Fath, Jean Dessès and, of course, Balmain.

One of the first things I learned was that everything at a couture house is made by hand. Even when a creaky old sewing machine is disdainfully used to reinforce the seams of a winter coat, those seams are first stitched by hand. Every garment, called a model and baptized with its own name while still in embryo form, is created to bring forth a new silhouette, a concept, fabric, or color combination. A couture house strives to stun the world.

With the original idea still in his head, the couturier sketches pages of variations. Then with his assistant close by, he begins draping yards and yards of unbleached muslin on a dressmaker's dummy; pinning, cutting, tucking, shaping until he's sure he's given birth to a new and exciting style. Only when the model looks like a winner does the designer convert his muslin pattern into the silk, wool, velvet, lace, or fur he had in mind all along.

At that point a live mannequin is summoned. "This will be for Jeanne; she's the tallest." Or "Only Suzanne can do justice to this low-cut neckline." Balmain was a perfectionist and would often spend ten or twelve hours draping and pinning before he was willing to let the dressmaker take over. If the mannequin showed any signs of fatigue he would fly into a rage. Sometimes he would ask me to watch. It was exhausting. Once when I had been unable to get away for either lunch or dinner, Art sent me a telegram: ROSES ARE RED, VIOLETS ARE BLUE, EVERY DAY I WORK HARDER THAN YOU.

At the end of my first month at Balmain, I was invited to behold a finished creation. "I want you to look, that's all," Pierre said. "Not a word to anyone downstairs; but you should know in advance what you'll be publicizing next season."

Each year Pierre Balmain, like all other members of the Haute Couture, designed 400 different models for women to wear every hour of the day or night. The first 200 were formally presented in late January for spring and summer; the second 200 in July for fall and winter.

In between, Pierre dashed off two mini collections; one in late November for "Le Ski" and another in late May for "La Saison"—the party-packed months of June and July.

As soon as one collection had been launched, Pierre would begin planning the next. He would linger around the salon for a week, watching the daily presentations, monitoring sales, checking press coverage, and then take a short vacation. A couple of weeks later he would appear unannounced, go to his desk, and reach for a new stack of sketch pads to start over again. And always with great exuberance. With a gleeful smile on his face, he would clap his hands and shout, "Let's start the scheduling!"

Scheduling meant setting up weeks of appointments with dozens of French manufacturers, from suppliers of fabrics and embroideries to leather craftsmen and jewelers. Pierre once ordered a special piece of 24-karat jewelry to cover the navel of a mannequin who would present his Garden of Eden bikini swimsuit. For another collection, he had a poodle dyed mauve to match a suit he was presenting and then ordered the dog a collar of real amethysts.

As soon as Balmain began working, a dense cloud of secrecy settled over the entire building. Competition among rival designers was legend and Eisenhower's plans for D-Day were no more guarded than Pierre's deliveries.

ART: **This was panic time in the couture house and I stayed away. Ann worked late into the night and her nerves were slightly frazzled because, from what she told me, everyone was screaming at each other and Balmain was at his grumpiest.**

One of the reasons was that although the clothes sold in the thousands of dollars, most of the couturiers with their fancy salons and hundreds of employees were always working on a razor-thin profit and one bad season could send them into bankruptcy. This was before they started putting their names on perfumes, cosmetics, T-shirts, and handbags. It was only after they began licensing their names for men's shaving lotion and underwear that they became rich.

Ann's major problem, as I recall at that time, was how to get the Duchess of Windsor to come to the openings. I told her it was simple—just give her a lot of free clothes.

"Who told you that?" she wanted to know.

"Elsa Maxwell—but you have to give her free clothes, too."

The week of the opening was a major event in Paris. Designers fought among themselves and with the Chambre Syndicale—the official group that somehow prevented fratricide among the dozens of high-strung artists—for their favorite show time. There were as many as six openings every day from 9:00 A.M. to 9:00 P.M. The fight to be the lead-off house was as heated as any major political campaign.

Four weeks before opening day, regular business changed dramatically. All clothes from the previous collection were placed on sale racks and reduced by a ratio of $100 per $1,000 of the original price. I was surprised to see many of our richest clients waiting for the doors to open on sale days. The most favored didn't even have to wait. They conspired with their favorite *vendeuse* so that the dress or suit they coveted would be hidden away for them. No matter that it was three months old and had been worn every afternoon in the three o'clock showing; it was gorgeous and reduced from $1,500 to $150.

As soon as the pandemonium of sale week subsided, all couture houses closed their doors to the public, and began a three-week race against time. A new collection had to be finished even if it meant working through the night. The couture house itself was given a face lift: walls were painted, gold chairs refurbished, chandeliers taken down and polished prism by prism, new draperies put up and new carpeting laid. One season Pierre decided to open a boutique where he would sell copies of his own custom-made clothes.

"Why should I let someone else knock off my designs when I can do the job better myself?" he explained as he ordered the rear wall of the ground floor ripped out, making space for one of the first ready-to-wear shops in the Couture. Within a year or two every other firm in Paris had a similar department.

Surrounded by scaffolding and hammering and cursing, I worked around the clock preparing press lists, invitations, releases, sketches for English-speaking journalists. Ginette Spanier, Balmain's sales director, worked even harder, luring private clients, Seventh Avenue manufacturers, store buyers, pattern companies, and all the celebrities listed in her secretly guarded black book.

On opening day, tired, hungry, but raring to go, all of us vied for front seats. Since the salon held only 200 people it was a tug of war. Ginette wanted her best customers in the front row, I wanted powerful members of the press seated there, and Balmain's business manager felt that his special contract people—pattern companies and foreign manufacturers who had paid $10,000 for copying rights—should be in the prime location. Oddly enough, the best front-row seat at every Balmain opening went to none of the above; it was reserved for Alice B. Toklas, Gertrude Stein's companion, critic, and housekeeper. Alice Toklas and Pierre were lifelong friends and he always waited nervously for her to appear. She invariably arrived late, walking with the strain of almost eighty years, wearing long, dull black clothing from the 1920s. Her impressions were very important to Pierre. When the collection ended and he'd taken his bow, he would whisk Miss Toklas over to a far corner of the salon for her critique of each model.

American reporters and buyers had a nonstop ball in Paris during the openings. After the first grueling week, they stayed on to see smaller showings, to photograph, sketch, buy accessories, and do follow-up stories. Every night was party time. Most of them spoke no French yet they lived in fear of being treated like tourists. Art and I were much in demand. And they all—from Mike Todd and Joan Crawford to advertising moguls and company presidents—requested the same thing: "We want to go where no other Americans have gone." Art once responded impatiently, "Okay, then go visit the garbage dump!" He knew every nook and cranny of Paris, and we wore ourselves to frazzles staying out until dawn with new and old friends.

Some first-timers were deceiving. I remember a slight, shy man who came to see the collection one afternoon at the end of opening week. He looked like an art student. He said he was from California and that Pierre, whom he'd met the night before at a party, had kindly reserved a seat for him in the front row. I noticed that he reached out and briefly touched every fabric whisking past him on the runway. When the collection was over, he came back to my office and handed me a scrap of paper, saying "Please thank Mr. Balmain, and in case he's forgotten my name since last night, here it is: James Galanos."

Another surprise was a fun-loving young New Yorker who a few years later was running his own collection as Bill Blass. Some old friends from America showed up, too. One of my favorites was a perky brunette whom I'd known at *Glamour* magazine. Her uncanny fashion sense had recently landed her a job as fashion director of Genesco Shoes. It seemed like the jackpot and we celebrated, neither of us dreaming that within two years Gerry Stutz would become president of Henri Bendel.

The grande dame of all the American editors was Carmel Snow of *Harper's Bazaar*. She could telephone a couture house, give a list of models she'd like to "take another look at," and have them delivered immediately to her workroom, which was a suite at the St. Regis Hotel. She stayed there in a large double bed, telephoning, scheduling photographs, making notes and plans until noon every day, dressed in a silk bed jacket, a breakfast tray by her side, her door open for deliveries, photographers, and publicity people until she was absolutely sure she had creamed the best for her Paris fashion issue.

ART: **Ann saw the Couture from the inside. I saw it from the outside. The fashion shows for the American buyers were held twice a year. Paris was still king as far as the U.S. dressmakers and department store buyers were concerned, and it provided me with plenty of material.**

For one thing everyone took it so seriously. I imagine it was a life or death matter whether Christian Dior would lower the skirt two inches or Jacques Fath would let the neck hit the navel. But to me it was just one big giggle. I would sit in the second or third row of an "opening" and stare with awe at the serious faces of these grown-up successful people taking notes as carefully as if they were students the day before finals.

My first reaction was to look over the fashion models. Most of them were too skinny for me and I don't recall

one who had what I considered an adequate bosom. A few times I would wander back to the dressing room, but the trip wasn't worth it because without clothes on, most of the models looked like boys. They also, with a few exceptions (the sisters Dorian Leigh and Suzy Parker), weren't too bright upstairs, and you couldn't have a conversation with them if you wanted to.

But the important thing was that in those days the Americans deferred to the French designers and whatever they came up with was what the American woman would wind up wearing for the next couple of years.

I recall writing one column about a Chanel suit. It was a very good-looking suit—so much so that in less than six months everyone in Paris was wearing it, including Ann. The column had to do with us having dinner together and I told her how much I admired it. She was pleased. Then I told her I had seen it on three women walking down the Champs-Élysées, a tour guide at the Eiffel Tower, twelve ladies cashing checks at American Express, and if I wasn't mistaken in the window of Air France where they were photographing four airline stewardesses. By the time the column ended the thrill of owning a Chanel suit, as far as Ann was concerned, was gone.

The trick of writing fashion columns was to treat them as seriously as Soviet-American Summit talks. The destiny of the Western world hung on what the couturiers would dream up for the following season.

As the designers got younger (a new one was discovered every year), I finally wrote about an eleven-year-old genius who had put the belt on the hips and hips on the belt. I reported that he was the next Yehudi Menuhin of fashion. When the spoof appeared in the U.S., several of the wire services received queries asking for more details on him as well as photos.

There was a lot of entertaining going on in those days and a lot of lonely women buyers. Before meeting up with Ann, I ate very well at Maxim's and the Grand Véfour on some major American department stores' lavish expense accounts—so the fashion openings weren't all bad.

After the openings were over and the American and foreign visitors left, my job took a different turn. For the next three months, we would try to get as much mileage out of Balmain's collection as possible. It was amazingly simple for one reason: I was the only English-speaking publicity girl in the industry. Whenever an American reporter or radio correspondent wanted a fashion feature, he called Balmain.

It was easy placing news items saying that Pierre had been commissioned to do all the costumes for an English play, or for a Noel Coward opening. Sometimes I had to hold back part of a story. For example, Marlene Dietrich insisted on having her fittings in the nude; in fact, I think she arrived for them wearing nothing but high-heeled sandals and a camel's-hair coat. Her appointments were always in the early morning, two hours before the house opened. I discovered this one day when I went into my office at 7:30 A.M., an unthinkable hour to the French, to rewrite a press release. As I crept up the stairs I heard giggling, coffee cups clinking, then a voice saying, "Wait outside, please." Out hustled a blushing fitter.

"What's going on in there?" I whispered.

Ginette stuck her head through the curtain and said, laughing, "Come on in and look at this gorgeous creature."

It was Marlene with her endless perfect legs swathed in a silk lace body suit embroidered with golden sequins and stars in three or four critical places—a vision. As soon as she had zippered it up, the fitter was summoned back to alter a tuck or two which Marlene swore were an eighth of an inch out of line. Marlene was her own best designer and fitter.

One morning shortly after that, Ginette whispered, "You have a guest in your office." Danny Kaye was sitting behind my desk, studiously reading our scrapbook.

"Clippings from Afghanistan, clippings from Wales, from Tasmania, from every city in South America—and not one from Missoula, Montana!" he shouted. "You're fired!"

Danny and his wife Sylvia were close friends of Ginette and her husband, Dr. Paul-Émile Seidman, whose double first name amused Danny. "How are you, darling Ginette, and how are Paul and Émile?" he would ask on his stopovers in Paris. Those nights we would gather at the Seidmans' and listen to Danny's songs and jokes until dawn.

ART: **I think it's only fair before we go any further to mention that there is going to be a lot of name dropping in this book. It's nobody's fault—it's just the way the French croissant crumbled while we lived in Paris. Ann met famous people while she worked for Pierre Balmain. I sought out others for my column. Many of them would have been unapproachable to us in the United States, but in Paris they were lost souls and the fact that a newspaperman wanted to talk to them gave them reassurance that they were not forgotten even for a few weeks.**

They not only held still for interviews but invited us to dinner, asked us to take them shopping and became good pals.

Paris was the "in" place to go in those days and by becoming friends with Betty and Humphrey Bogart, we became friends with Elizabeth Taylor and Mike Todd who sent us Gene Kelly who sent us Cary Grant etc. etc. and ad infinitum, not to mention Alfred Hitchcock and Grace Kelly.

I became the unofficial American greeter to Americans in Paris and loved every moment of it. Whenever

someone said "I'm going to Paris" the other person would reply "You must look up the Buchwalds."

The ones I remember with the most warmth were Fred Allen, who had been a hero of my youth; Betty and Bogie; Nunnally Johnson, the screenwriter; Lena Horne, a woman for whom I always lusted in my heart; Dinah Shore; Lew and Edie Wasserman (he's now chairman of MCA); Betsy Grant, one of Cary's wives; Gene and Betsy Kelly; Al Capp (we eventually wound up not being friends); and Faye Emerson, a TV rocket of the 50s. There were many others, not necessarily famous names.

One of my favorite visiting firemen stories had to do with a fellow who called me up and said a Harold Simmons told him as soon as he got to Paris to give me a ring. I invited him to lunch at Fouquet's. "How's good old Harold?" I asked.

"I don't know Harold," he said. "I know Sam Kraslow who knows Harold."

"I don't know Kraslow," I said.

"You're not missing much," the man said.

We got along fine and I decided to play a joke on Simmons. I asked the man to go to Simmons' office with a letter from me introducing the person as a personal French friend of mine who had never been to New York. I asked Simmons to show the Frenchman the "21" Club, the Statue of Liberty, and take him shopping at Macy's.

The man did it and Simmons refused to see him, telling him through his secretary he was too busy to entertain my French friends.

But most of the people who came were very nice and Paris was and is still our bond. We were all young and gay—the price was right and even twenty years later

we all get misty eyed when we talk about a dinner or a boat ride down the Seine.

The important thing though is, that, if the book is weighted down with names it's only because we were in the center of the tourist hurricane that hit Europe in the late forties and fifties, and since I was the only American writing a column in Europe at the time it stood to reason that these were the people who played a part of our Paris life.

Besides there is some question if anyone would be interested if we wrote we were responsible for Zetta Goldberg marrying Harvey Zimmerman in the 16th Arrondissement on a spring day in 1954.

Many aspects of my job at Balmain were far from glamorous. When I first had arrived I learned that the publicity files contained less than thirty listings and only four American newspapers.

When I checked with Pierre, he said, "But they're the very best American papers: the New York *Times*, the New York *Herald Tribune*, the Dallas *Morning News*, and, oh yes, my favorite, the *Capitol Times* in Madison, Wisconsin."

"But Mr. Balmain, there are forty-eight states in the U.S. and each has a capital, and each capital city has a morning and usually an evening paper; that means we should have at least ninety-six journals on the lists."

He was thunderstruck and asked if by chance I knew a woman he had been consistently kicking out of the collections because she claimed to represent 4,000 papers.

"Of course she's lying," he added.

"What are her papers called?" I asked.

"She says it is the Ass-o-ciated Press, ha ha."

"I burst out laughing. Even with my limited experience I knew then that I could handle my job. Ten minutes later I was at the post office sending a telegram to Marihelen MacDuff, my closest friend at Neiman-Marcus and the store's publicity director: PLEASE RUSH LIST

OF FASHION EDITORS MAJOR NEWSPAPERS STOP JUST LANDED JOB PUBLICITY DIRECTOR PIERRE BALMAIN AM SCARED STIFF.

Within a week Marihelen airmailed a mile-long list of every newspaper, magazine, wire service, or throwaway newsletter in the world. I immediately told my secretary to type a separate card for each listing. When I left Balmain two years later, she was still working on the assignment and to this day, no one in Paris realizes that Balmain's publicity office houses a mailing list worth its weight in gold.

But Balmain had no budget for the kind of worldwide mailings most American publicity offices consider essential. My real function was to create news that would attract the attention of papers and news bureaus with Paris branch offices. It worked.

One day in early 1950 an Associated Press reporter called excitedly to say that he had just interviewed Elizabeth Taylor and her new husband Nicky Hilton. They were spending a week in Paris on their honeymoon and he had a swell idea. "Elizabeth said she had never owned a Paris dress. What do you think about Pierre Balmain making one for her?" I checked my watch; only ten minutes before lunch. I hurried to Pierre's office and explained the plan, adding that everything would have to be done while the house was closed. Elizabeth insisted that no one be around to watch. I begged him to sacrifice his lunch date with his mother, just this one time, so that we could hit a thousand newspapers. He gave in, I telephoned the reporter, and within ten minutes Elizabeth and the AP correspondent appeared in Pierre's office.

Elizabeth, so young and beautiful she would have looked glamourous in a scruffy wool bathrobe, said meekly, "Mr. Balmain, I've never been allowed to wear a really slinky dress; do you suppose you could make me one, in pink if possible?"

Pierre nodded, reached for a bolt of delicate wool, light as chiffon, and looking at his watch, said, "Let's go. Take off your dress and stand still." As he began to drape the fabric around Elizabeth, who stood obediently straight as a soldier in a white, lace-trimmed slip, Pierre gasped, "You're not wearing a girdle!"

"I NEVER wear a girdle!" said Elizabeth.

"Then no slinky dress," Pierre snapped as he stopped draping.

Elizabeth gazed longingly at what she saw in the three-way mirror, hesitated for a few seconds, then said, "I love it; all my life I've had to wear silly, little-girl dresses. Okay, I'll put on a girdle, if you have one."

Pierre snapped his fingers at me. "Ann, the shop across the street is open until one P.M. Go get a panty girdle, size small, and charge it."

I walked into the lingerie shop just as the owner was flipping her door sign from OUVERTE to FERMÉ, grabbed one of the few American panty girdles she had in stock, and ran back to Balmain.

Pierre cut and basted a dramatic one-shoulder evening gown while Elizabeth stood motionless as a professional model. Within an hour the AP photographer took a thirty-six-roll of black and white photos, the best of which ran for weeks in thousands of papers around the world. In fact, the photo of Pierre Balmain making Elizabeth Taylor's first Paris dress had a longer life than her marriage to Nicky Hilton.

ART: **A short note here. I was covering the Taylor-Hilton honeymoon for my column. The first night they hit town Hilton left Elizabeth in her suite and went out on the town to prowl. I couldn't believe it. Here was the current world sex symbol spending the first night of her honeymoon alone in the George V. It made me lose faith not only in sex symbols, but Hilton hotels as well.**

Another American visitor who directed the spotlight to Balmain was Edgar Bergen. He arrived from California with two crates containing his famous dolls, Charlie McCarthy and a new female character, Podine Puffington, for whose début he wanted a Paris dress. French Customs refused to give the dolls clearance, and an outcry from the press put us on the front page even before Pierre saw the gawky Podine. When at last we convinced Customs to release the ventriloquist's dummy, Pierre had only twenty-four hours to dream up a dress, and I even less time to arrange maximum press coverage. We pulled it off, however; reporters and photographers poured into the salon for the unveiling. As Pierre worked down to the wire, Edgar Bergen enthralled them with hours of his most successful television routines. Just as his voice was about to give out, Pierre marched in with the dress and we again made front-page news.

Later that spring, Ginette Spanier received a call from London. "Gorgeous" Gussie Moran had arrived from the States and had her heart set on a Paris-designed tennis dress for her first Wimbledon match; would Pierre be interested? Gussie Moran was called Gorgeous because of her beautiful long legs and because of the tennis outfits she wore. She was then ranked fourth among U. S. women players and was the first woman contender to reject plain white shorts and the starched gym suit look for a tennis DRESS. Now she wanted a Paris creation. Pierre said, "I have it! We'll make this Gussie really gorgeous in a tennis dress of white chiffon and lace; it will float like a cloud, we'll put lace on the panties too!"

Our press coverage was massive. I took the finished work of art to London the week before Wimbledon started, and reporters filled the banquet hall of the Dorchester Hotel photographing Gussie having her final fitting. We received clippings from all over the world. Gussie didn't win at Wimbledon that Spring but I did.

ART: **Among the many arguments Ann and I had in her Balmain days is that I refused to touch a publicity stunt she was associated with. Balmain knew of our relationship as did everyone else in her shop and they were all perplexed that Ann's stories could never get in the column. Ann understood the conflict of interest but she was still infuriated by the dead silence. "If it's a legitimate publicity story," she argued, "I should get as much consideration as anyone else."**

I told her, "There is no such thing as a legitimate

publicity story, unless Gussie Moran decided to play in no shorts at all."

That night I found myself tapping on Ann's window in my French Marshall's hat—but she wouldn't let me in.

My greatest publicity coup came about totally by accident. One afternoon I wandered across the Champs-Élysées and with no appointment walked into the office of David Schoenbrun, who was head of CBS in France. His friends included everyone from Charles de Gaulle on down. I had never met Schoenbrun and was nervously biting my lip as I introduced myself as the publicity director of Pierre Balmain.

"I know I should have called first, but I was afraid you'd laugh," I said apologetically. "Here's my request. Since television seems to be growing fast in the United States, I'd like to know if you and I could plan some fashion features."

David bolted out from behind his desk, gave me a big hug, and said, "We've been trying to work with the French Couture for three years! They won't let us in the door, everyone treats radio correspondents like spies; come on up to the press bar; this deserves a drink, Ann McGarry."

As television quickly graduated from wrestling matches to less sweaty entertainment, David Schoenbrun and I made Balmain's name a household word in the United States. When Ed Murrow asked for a Paris feature for his Easter Parade special, it was Balmain's millinery collection. And when Jack Benny and his wife Mary visited Paris, they were photographed at Pierre's collection.

One of the few things about my job which always plagued me were the press releases. Often I would beg Art for help and once he gave me the following on a Balmain letterhead:

For Immediate Publication

Pierre Balmain revealed today that his collection was one of the worst he has made, and that he has decided to give up his business and open a quick-lunch restaurant in the Champs-Élysées area.

"There has long been a need for a fine restaurant in this quarter," said the couturier, "And since dress designers are a dime a dozen in town, I have decided I'm not good enough to compete with any of them.

"It has always been my contention that no design on earth can save a woman who has a bad figure," said Balmain, "and I think—have always thought—that a woman is a fool to spend $400 or $500 on a dress just because it is a little different. Clothes were made to keep people warm; it's ridiculous the lengths to which women go to look smart.

"I believe," he continued, "that my restaurant will be the best in Paris; I dare Jacques Fath or Christian Dior to open one next to it!"

At times Art seemed as irreverent about his own job as he was about mine. One morning he called me at Balmain around 10:30 in the morning. He sounded only half-awake. I was terribly busy—three reporters were arguing at my desk—so I said, "Get up, Art, and go to work!" and hung up. Thirty minutes later the telephone rang again. It was Art who said, "I'm at the office like you told me! Now what do I do?"

ART: **This seems to be as good a time as any to tell about my work in those days. I was responsible for writing four columns a week—the titles changing all the time. One was "Paris After Dark" which concerned itself with reviewing nightclubs and restaurants. The restaurant idea was my own. Nightclubs in Paris, as anywhere, are drags to write about. A singer is good or no good and if he or she is no good why waste space to say so. The big shows such as the Lido and the Bal Tabarin went on for a year without changing. The Russian boîtes with viol-**

inists playing in your ear and drinking your champagne had a certain romantic atmosphere if you were willing to pay the price. And the late spots such as Jimmy's on the Left Bank and Bricktop's on the Right could be dispensed with in a couple of columns.

But restaurants were another matter. Everyone who came to Paris had to, and wanted to eat. I therefore designated myself the wine and food critic of the Paris *Herald Tribune*. My credentials for this job were superb. I had been in the Marines for four years and dined on military cuisine, then went to USC for three years where I ate in the student union, and finally I spent six months eating Polish sausages at the Hôtel des États-Unis.

But Eric Hawkins, the managing editor, was happy to have someone reviewing restaurants particularly since it brought in far more mail than anything I had to say about nightclubs.

The letters were usually tips from readers who had a favorite restaurant in Paris that they thought I should be made aware of. There were so many that it would have taken a lifetime as well as a new liver to get through them all. Every night I went to a different spot, taking copious notes and faking it as to what was good and what wasn't. But when it comes to eating in Paris you have to learn something and pretty soon I could tell a good sauce from a lousy one and even the difference between Burgundy and Bordeaux. (Burgundy came in the long bottle and Bordeaux came in the squat one.)

In no time at all I was the American expert of French food, and since the French were catering to American tourists in those days, a writeup in the *Herald Tribune* could do wonders for an out-of-the-way bistro.

I recall writing up a place called l'Ours Martin on the

quai d'Alma once. That evening friends said, "Let's go to the restaurant you wrote up in your column." I called and an irritable lady said in French, "Sorry, we're all full up."

"But," I protested, "I'm the fellow who wrote about you in the *Herald Tribune* today."

"Yes," she said. "That's why we're all full up" and slammed down the phone on me.

Once Darryl Zanuck called me and said, "Give me the name of a restaurant no Americans go to."

I told him, "Chez l'Ami Louis by the Bastille."

Two nights later I walked in and everyone from 20th Century-Fox who happened to be in Paris at the time was seated at one of the tables.

Spyros Skouras, the chairman, said to me, "How come you found out about Darryl's favorite restaurant?"

Besides "Paris After Dark" I reviewed French and American films. The French were the toughest because I didn't understand them. In fairness to the picture the less I understood the dialogue, the better review I gave it, figuring even if I got the plot wrong the producer wouldn't complain.

The other column was "Paris and People." Originally it was in diary form and written by five people. They all disappeared and a fellow reporter named Robert Yoakum and I took it over. Then he went off to work for an organization called the World Veterans Federation which was supposed to be devoted to preventing another war.

So I inherited the column and the $50 a week that went with it. I began by doing interviews, but eventually shifted to humorous features about fun and games in Europe.

No one paid too much attention to what I was doing and no one on the *Herald Tribune* gave me any trouble unless I asked for more money.

Art still did better at raising his salary than I did. My paycheck at Balmain never rose over $25 a week, about 12,500 francs, and even that was handed to me under the table. There was no way for the French government to issue me a work permit. I assume I was listed as an office supply by Balmain's business manager, who thought publicity itself was meaningless and that an American employee was folly. We exchanged angry words every Friday night when I went to be reimbursed for my business expenses—lunches with editors, drinks with reporters, cabs to photo assignments. He capitulated eventually but only after months of unusually high sales following a flurry of press clippings. We became friends in a distant, wary manner.

Because Pierre acknowledged that $25 a week was a sorry salary, albeit the best he could offer, he gave me a bonus. Every season he made me an entire wardrobe: a daytime dress, a suit with two or three blouses, a cocktail dress and/or suit, and a coat.

When I went out for an unusually elegant evening, Pierre encouraged me to borrow from the collection. He said it was good advertising. But fitting the evening dresses became a joke. I learned to shorten hems as much as ten inches by Scotch-taping them to petticoats. I stuffed cotton, tissue, or even old press releases into tops of strapless dresses designed on mannequins with Raquel Welch bosoms. During dinner one night in a restaurant, a twenty-inch zipper simply opened its tiny teeth and each side went its own way, baring my back from neckline to buttocks. I borrowed Art's suit jacket, wore it throughout dinner with a group of very dressed-up Americans, and when it came time to leave managed to dash from table to exit in two steps.

ART: **Until I read this it didn't occur to me at the time why Ann was so well clothed. I never bothered to ask where**

she got her clothes. I guess I just assumed that all American girls from Warren, Pennsylvania, were dressed by someone like Pierre Balmain.

My most embarrassing accident with a borrowed dress happened while I was dancing with Pierre one night at Chez Carrère. Pierre, who was a superb dancer, had just returned from a business trip to South America. He was determined to teach me a new dance, the Mambo. As I twisted around, the thin spaghetti straps on my dress ripped and the entire top of the dress slid down around my hips. I froze. Pierre whispered calmly, "Just turn and face me." Then he magically whisked out two straight pins from behind the lapel of his dinner jacket, reached over my shoulders, retrieved first one strap, then the other, and quickly pinned them to the front of my dress. One, perhaps two seconds was all it took. Pierre's feet hadn't missed a beat.

I gulped in amazement. "How did you happen to have PINS?"

"I never go out without them," he said, "even in white tie and tails."

Much as I loved every item of my Balmain wardrobe, I did a terrible thing. I covered my living expenses by selling them all at the end of each season to a small blonde Australian journalist. The only difficulty came when I had to tell Pierre about the tragic loss of each of the garments. After six or seven seasons, it was almost impossible to think of new fibs. "You'll never believe what that dry cleaner did to my jersey dress—bleached it!" "They stole my coat right from under my nose at that rotten restaurant" or "I did it again, put a hot iron smack in the middle of my velvet jacket, ruined it!" Once I actually dumped a bottle of mustard on the front of a black cocktail dress, let it dry to a convincing cakiness, took it up to Pierre's office for its last rites, then rushed back to my apartment, washed off the mustard, dried and pressed the dress perfectly, and handed it to my benefactress the following morning.

I think Pierre knew what I was doing, and in a certain way enjoyed my agonized lamentations, if not the loss of his clothes. He had specified at the start that I was to put my wardrobe on the sale rack at the end of each season so the firm could recuperate a small part of its original cost. But he never said more than "C'est la vie" or "Quel dommage!" as he changed the subject to some flaw he detected in whatever new dress or suit I was breaking in. "Go have your hem shortened," he would order. "You're wearing it two centimeters too long." Or, "You still haven't learned how to tie a good bow; ask Suzanne to give you another lesson."

I'm certain he never believed a syllable of my sad explanations.

ART: **As I read the above I couldn't for the life of me remember where I got my clothes. I believe I bought most of my suits in London off the rack at Simpson's Department Store on Piccadilly. Once I had shirts made for me in Italy for about $10 each. I also had a pair of shoes made for me in Barcelona. I remember this well because I couldn't take the shoes with me. The shoemaker promised to mail them one at a time so I wouldn't have to pay duty on them. In about a month the customs people called me. There was a shoe in each box, one had been posted a week before the other but the French had waited patiently for the other before making me pay full duty. The French customs official said, "We always wait for the second shoe when one arrives from Spain."**

Whenever Pierre was invited to present his collections I traveled with him—to Biarritz, New York, Monte Carlo, London, even to Amsterdam where we spent three extra days after the mannequins returned to Paris because a Dutch manufacturer signed Pierre for a ready-to-wear line adapted from his original models. One night we rented a boat to tour the canals. I was fascinated as we floated by the red light district. Grinning, fat prostitutes dressed in red satins and laces sat in their front windows, flirting with potential customers staring up from the streets. One woman in particular stands out in my memory: her hair was dyed the same bright red as her dress, and she was knitting bright red baby booties.

Often my travels included a bit of smuggling for Pierre, usually costumes for London plays. He did a lot of this work as Ginette had a vast circle of London theater friends and was an expert at enticing producers and directors to Balmain's showroom.

Frequently the work took longer than planned to finish, or the play would open a week earlier than scheduled. Only an airplane could get the dresses to London in time, and Pierre assigned me the job of sneaking them through Customs.

My worst experience was the day I had to deliver an outfit to Hildegarde, then one of the most popular cabaret singers in the world. She was six feet tall, and for her opening at the Palladium she had ordered a brilliant emerald satin strapless evening gown with a matching full-length satin coat. As I approached the Customs agent with my battered American suitcase, I prayed that my luck would hold. If he should question the contents ("Really, miss, emerald satin to go sightseeing in?") and ask me to put them on to prove they were my size, I would look like a collapsed green tent. Fortunately, the agent just said, "Have a fine weekend, miss." I couldn't even smile "thanks" I was so afraid I'd be sick all over his Arrivals Ledger.

When I told Art about it that night—I stayed only long enough to rush my contraband to Hildegarde's hotel, then flew back to Paris—he raged.

"Promise me. Never again! I'll tell Pierre myself—one more smuggling job and you quit! Besides," he added, "you didn't even take a toothbrush for a night in jail."

I kept my promise to Art with one exception: years later a close friend, hearing Art and I were on our way to New York, asked me to bring over a Chanel suit she'd ordered before she left Paris. "No problem," I wrote back, and immediately picked it up from Chanel's workroom. Because it was such a splendidly embroidered work of art, I packed it lovingly on top of my own clothes, swathing it in tissue like a sultan's robe. As we headed for the airport on the day of our departure, Art asked, "You're not smuggling anything, are you? Tell the truth now."

And I answered, "I told you my smuggling was only for Balmain emergencies."

It sufficed until we began to unpack. Art had bought us matching luggage and he opened mine by mistake: there lay my friend's suit, blouse, necklace, belt, even a personal note from Chanel to her!

ART: **This friend, whom I love dearly, was a born smuggler, as long as someone else did it for her. She certainly could afford the duty on anything she bought, but that would take the fun out of buying a Paris creation.**

Years after this particular incident when Ann and I were living in Washington, we went to Paris on a visit. As soon as we checked into the Hôtel George V the phone rang. My friend had tracked us down and had a little item waiting for her at Schlumberger, the great Paris jeweler. Would Ann mind picking it up and stuffing it into her pantyhose?

Fortunately I answered the phone and told her, "You're out of your gourd."

"Let me speak to Annie," she said brusquely.

"No way," I said. "I can't make bail for her and also take her to Lassere tonight."

"All right, I'll pay the lousy duty. Just bring it back for me."

"No way. You'll declare it for $2,000 and some sneaky French Schlumberger employee will tell U.S. Customs it's worth $10,000, and I'll be doing five years on Alcatraz while you wear your bauble to the Academy Awards."

When I hung up Ann was embarrassed.

"She asks so little of us."
"Yeh, like paying a $50,000 fine."

I missed one trip back to the States by five minutes, and cried for an hour, not because I wanted to see the newly built Fontainebleau Hotel in Miami but because I was homesick and had plotted to meet my mother and sister Jeanne in New York.

Pierre had planned to take his assistant Eric on the trip, but eight days before the departure date, he called me into his office to say that it seemed unlikely Eric would receive his passport in time. "So," said Pierre, "you will have to accompany me. Now let's get started on a wardrobe for you, a tweed cape and skirt I think. . . . "

How I hated that tweed cape! Pierre was introducing a new longer length, and the cape fell to the top of my shoes. I looked like Toulouse-Lautrec's little sister.

A week later, as the taxi pulled up in front of Balmain's where Pierre and I were waiting on the curb, our luggage piled beside us, Ginette Spanier opened the salon window above us and screamed down, "Hold everything, Eric's passport came through! A police car is rushing it here, there's the siren now. Eric is on his way down, bon voyage, Monsieur Balmain, bon voyage, Eric!" And off went the two men before I could stoop to pick up my valise and lug it back up the stairs to my office. My only consolation was that I didn't have to wear that tweed.

ART: **Thinking Ann had left, I was in the process of making other social plans while she was away. But fortunately they never got put into effect. It was a good lesson for me. Don't do anything rash when your lady leaves town until you get a confirmation from the airline that the plane has landed at its final destination.**

When I finally did get to go to the States with Pierre I was so excited at the prospect of seeing my family I had trouble keeping my mind on work. My mother dropped everything in Warren and came to New York to greet me, then stayed on with my sister Jeanne in her apartment while Pierre and I darted in and out of New York on a whirlwind tour of Eastern and Southern cities. Balmain was fêted at every stop on our schedule. Wherever we went the city's social leaders gave parties in his honor. One hostess openly admitted to redecorating her living room for the luncheon we were attending. As we were leaving her house she drew me aside and asked anxiously, "Do you think Mr. Balmain liked the color of my new draperies? The men finished hanging them just an hour before you arrived."

During rest stops in Manhattan, I spent hours talking to my mother about my work, my travels in Europe, my life in Paris, about everything except the true status of my relationship with Art. I read aloud funny parts of Art's letters which arrived daily from London where he had gone scouting for column material. But I couldn't find a way to tell my mother that Art had become the most important part of my life. How could I explain our crazy days and wondrous nights, then admit to a blank space for the future? She listened with delight, never interrupting or questioning, just loving me. I could do no wrong in her eyes, and I knew I owed her more than jokes and travelogues. "I hope to marry him," I finally blurted out. My sister Jeanne had also been listening and she gasped in dismay. But my mother merely nodded and said, "I know. And if that's what you want, you'll work it out some way."

I wrote to Art daily. "Oh, honey, I'm so tired of rushing around," I complained. "These days of waiting to return seem endless. I don't ever want to leave you again for such a long time. . . . "

Still, my first year with Art ended with nothing resolved, but as my plane broke through the gloomy clouds over Paris I suddenly realized I'd not only survived a year in Paris, but I was returning to begin a second, this one even more unpredictable than the first.

Three

Nineteen fifty-one was the year Art and I didn't get married. Time and again we didn't get married.

When Balmain and I returned from our month in New York in mid-December, Pierre had exactly six weeks to create a spring collection scheduled for the end of the coming month. His deadline seemed a fitting one for me to appropriate as the date when I would make a decision about my own future. If, by the time American buyers and reporters arrived for the January collections, Art and I were still in the same holding pattern, I would pass the word among those I trusted that I was ready for a stateside job. With their help something would surely materialize. My heart hurt at the thought of ever leaving Art, but I knew that if I so much as hinted about my plan it would sound like an ultimatum.

It was therefore with some relief that I accompanied Pierre to England ten days before Christmas. We were showing a raincoat collection to a British manufacturer. The weather in London was perfect; it rained every day. Drenched and depressed, I sloshed around for two days until we returned to Paris by boat-train, in time to go to the opening of the American Ballet.

As I was dressing, a thermometer in my mouth for reassurance that my face was flushed with anticipation rather than fever, Art burst into my room. "Wait til you hear what happened to me after yesterday's column," he said.

The day before he'd written about Cartier, choosing it as a good pre-Christmas topic. The Cartier people were so pleased they invited him to the place Vendôme and presented him with a silver cigarette case and lighter, the case engraved: "To Art Buchwald, Cartier's historian."

Art rarely smoked cigarettes and since he lost anything not chained to his body, I said jokingly, "I'll be glad to take care of them for you."

"No, I found something else for you while I was in Cartier's," he said and handed me a red velvet box with an engagement ring inside—an elegant spiral of gold set with tiny diamonds.

"Is it real?" I screamed and put it on my ring finger to wear to the ballet. On our way we stopped at the Hôtel George V to have a drink with Mervyn Leroy, the movie director. To this day he is the only other person who ever saw that ring. As we sat waiting for Mervyn, Art said, "I've thought about this for months; we'll be married by a priest." I couldn't believe that all our past religious differences had suddenly vanished, so I asked fearfully, "And if someday a curly-headed kid who looks just like you were to attend Mass every Sunday, will that be okay?" Art answered, "I know it's going to be tough, but I think it'll be good for us. Neither of us knows anything about smooth roads."

ART: **I think I remember this. It sounds rather gauche that I accepted the cigarette case from Cartier's but they had engraved it to me and I felt I would hurt their feelings if I didn't. Since I didn't smoke cigarettes I rationalized it wasn't a bribe, although when I look back on it what the hell was it? I had done a story on Cartier's in Paris. Without using real names it included some anecdotes**

about the place. My favorite had to do with a lady who came in one day and looked at a $30,000 diamond bracelet. She told the salesman she would be back on two occasions and would have a different man in tow on each of them. The salesman was to tell each man when she said she wanted the bracelet that it only cost $15,000.

Sure enough a week later she came in with one gentleman, priced out the bracelet at $15,000—returned a few days later and did the same with another man. Both paid $15,000 and the bracelet was hers.

The story as you may have guessed was that one man was her lover—the other her husband. Both now believed they had bought her the bracelet and she could wear it at all times without any explanations.

Anyway when they handed me the cigarette case, on impulse I asked to see their engagement rings and they showed me something in the three- or four-hundred-dollar range. On impulse again I said I'd buy one and pay at the end of the month. Then on a third impulse I gave it to Ann—as described in her version.

I learned a lot from all this. One was never to accept a silver cigarette case from a jeweler, even if he had it engraved in advance—and secondly, if you do there is no need to buy an engagement ring from him just because you feel guilty.

For a couple of days after I got the ring, we discussed when we would tell our families. Then one night at a little neighborhood restaurant, Art suddenly declared that he would break his father's heart if he married a Gentile. We kept talking until I was in tears, weeping all over the Chinese food neither of us had touched. I recalled a heated discussion months previously when I'd stated my belief that all grown people must finally take a stand on religion and that by evading the issue Art was surely going to suffer someday. But I never dreamed he'd begin thinking only after we were engaged. Art said even though he never practiced his religion, he didn't want to sacrifice it for another one, mine. For good measure, he added that his father would probably disown him. I cried as much for the tough spot he was in as for myself.

When we got home that night I offered to give back his ring. He took it and left without a word. Actually, I threw it at him and pushed him out of my room. I was still sobbing hours later when Art stomped angrily back, threatening violence if I wouldn't put the ring on again. So I did.

The next morning he knocked on my door around noon. It was obvious he hadn't slept all night. He said he couldn't resolve the religious problem. He didn't understand about God or why it mattered that he try to. He was so upset he kept running between my room and the bathroom at the end of the hall to vomit. It was almost funny but we were both dreadfully sad. When at last he stopped throwing up, he took the darned ring and this time he kept it, muttering, "I probably couldn't have paid for it anyway." That did it; I would head for New York as soon as possible. But Art, insisting he still had more things to talk over with me, followed me to my office. We stopped at a little bar across the street where between dashes to the men's room he related a new fear. If he married me his children would go to Catholic schools where nuns and priests would wean them away from him.

"I don't want to be left out," he said. "I don't want my kids to ever look at me as if I didn't know the score."

I tried to explain that indeed they would go to Mass, learn their Catechism, and be Confirmed but that they'd also have a few minutes left over each day to talk to their father.

ART: **This thing was getting to be a bitch. All the things I told Ann about my family were true. But there was a lot more to it than that. I had been raised in foster homes in Hollis, New York, for the most part, which was not a**

Jewish neighborhood. The kids that bugged the few Jews who lived there the most were the ones who went to parochial school.

My experiences with these Catholic kids when I was young were not pleasant ones, and I think somewhere in the back of my mind I had a nightmare that if I had kids and they were raised Catholic they would beat me up.

I also felt if they were raised Catholic they wouldn't really be mine. The church would have first dibs on them and I would come in a poor second.

Because I have always had a vivid imagination I kept replaying scenes that could or would happen. Whatever Jewish upbringing I had—and it wasn't very intense—taught me Gentiles were the enemy and the surest way to hell was to marry one.

I'm certain Ann had very little experience with Jewish men before she met me, yet in all our years of marriage our different faiths have never been a problem. But at the time it loomed as a terrible one. That and the simple fact that I wasn't sure I wanted to get married made me into one miserable person.

Art finally left the bar and went home to sleep, my ring back in his pocket again. Nothing had been settled. Despite my vow to leave Paris, I couldn't walk out on Balmain before his spring collection. It was a critical one. His previous showing had not been a roaring success. In fact, sales had been so disappointing that his business manager had summoned me to his office to say sadly, "Unfortunately, we will not be able to pay all salaries this month, yours included, but just this month, you understand. We are having temporary financial problems and you will be responsible for denying this regrettable fact if anyone asks about it. Not one word should leak out to the press or the public."

I knew February press promotion would be vitally important to the house and dug into my work, postponing all decisions. I continued seeing Art every night while he vacillated between wanting to get married and wishing that he were free.

Art's ambivalence led to another abortive marriage attempt in the early spring. Late one afternoon he burst into my room waving a letter he had just received.

"We can get married in Echternach!" he announced victoriously.

An American woman named Treiweiler, married to a dentist in Echternach, had bombarded Art with letters begging him to visit Echternach as their house guest and do a column on their annual religious festival. That morning Art had called Mrs. Treiweiler. She sounded young, terrific, someone we'd both like, he told me. The festival would be a wonderful weekend.

"You jump for four hours without stopping," Art added as if that would be an inducement. We had both been invited, but best of all, Art said, Mrs. Treiweiler had promised that it would be a cinch for her to arrange for us to get married while we were there. I didn't ask Art why Mrs. Treiweiler had thrown in marriage as part of the invitation, because I could almost hear him saying that he would come only if he could bring me with him, but that we weren't married yet because of French bureaucracy.

Pierre Balmain okayed my request for a four-day weekend, and off we went to a town we could barely pronounce. Echternach claimed to be the center of European Christianity. Founded in 732 A.D., it went along its pagan way until an old priest named Father Willibrod converted the whole area to Catholicism in one fell swoop. He was later canonized Saint Willibrod due to a miracle the townspeople had celebrated ever since.

In 756 A.D. a Catholic convert named Veit took off with his wife on a pilgrimage to Rome, and stayed away so long he was presumed dead. His relatives stole his property and divided it among themselves. One sunny morning Veit suddenly reappeared, announcing sorrowfully that his wife had been killed by robbers on the way home. His relatives, afraid to admit that they had confiscated his property, decided to frame him instead. They told the town council Veit had killed his wife, and should be hanged.

As poor Veit was mounting the scaffold he asked for a final request: the right to play one last tune on his violin. It was granted. As he began to play, the people began dancing, and unable to stop, were still dancing twelve hours later. Even the cattle danced. Fearful that they would all drop dead with fatigue, the people prayed to their beloved Father Willibrod saying that if he would allow them to rest they would dance each year in thanksgiving. Within moments they stopped. Meanwhile old Veit just walked down from the scaffold, the story goes, and disappeared into the hills never to be seen again. Some end the story by swearing St. Vitus dance originated that day, but there are no records to prove it.

When Art and I arrived in Echternach on Friday night, its population had swollen from 3,000 inhabitants to a town jammed with 17,000 people. Promptly at 8:00 A.M. the next morning they all formed lines of five abreast, and holding hands, piously began to jump up and down. A mile and a half of humanity jumped through the cobblestoned streets, through the entire town, out into the surrounding fields, and finally through the church and out its back door. The ritual went on for precisely four hours. Whoever completed the entire four hours without stopping or falling down would receive whatever special request he was praying for.

I wrote to my mother on our return to Paris: "I did it, my first jumping Novena, and am still stiff after five days. Art appointed me to do the jumping while he took photos which we will send you as soon as I can squeeze into shoes and go to the photo store."

Art and I were the only Americans there, except for our hostess who couldn't jump because she was so busy trying to get us married. We lacked every necessary paper including our birth certificates. Which made it very clear to me that Art went to Echternach for good column material, not to get married. When I accused him of this, he just grinned and hugged me. But it was a unique weekend.

We hiked, biked, and picnicked through every foot of Luxembourg hills, until Art got diarrhea from drinking too much raw country milk, and returned home slim and svelte from living in the Treiweilers' bathroom our last two days.

ART: **I gave it a good try in Echternach. I really was prepared to get married there and I did dance, though not for five hours. The fact that we couldn't get married was not my fault. The fact the festival made an excellent piece for the paper was also not my fault.**

We have to keep all this in perspective. Nobody seemed to want to marry us, and there didn't seem to be any rush about it as far as I was concerned. But the column was due and I had to write from where I was. Had I not gotten a column out of our trip and also not been able to get married—*then* I really would have been disappointed.

Back in Paris I forced myself to make some decisions. If Art wanted to keep playing games, I would show him! I'd find a job in New York and disappear without telling him.

Out of the blue I received a telegram offering me the position of fashion director in a Seventh Avenue buying office—I accepted by return cable. That night, getting ready to go out with Art, I was so nervous I could barely fasten my dress. Although I was convinced I'd done the right thing, my fears increased with every second. I was only slightly consoled by a vision of Art's desolation when he called some morning the next week only to find that I had gone for good.

Art knocked on my door at eight o'clock and we went to meet Betty and Bogey at the Ritz Bar. We were going to celebrate their return from the jungle where Bogey had just finished *The African Queen*. When we walked in, Betty was sitting alone in one of the side booths. The maître d' whispered to Art, "Mr. Bogart is having a massage and wants you to go up to his room." Art nodded. "You go sit with Betty. Bogey and I'll be down in a few minutes." So I slid into the booth next to her, again amazed at her astonishing beauty.

After I'd ordered a drink, we stared at each other for a few minutes and then she said disgustedly, "You're sure a lot of laughs tonight . . . what's wrong?"

She's the one person I can tell, I thought. I'll never see her again. Besides, she couldn't care less and I must tell someone or I'll burst. So, leaning closer, I began.

"I don't feel very happy tonight, in fact I feel like crying but I promise I won't. I've just accepted a job in New York and I'm going to take it. I'll just leave without telling Art a word. I've thought it out and I know I'm right! Art will always need to be free. We're opposites in every way, not only in religion but . . ."

As I talked I felt more and more like Joan of Arc buying matches in case the pyre went out, a martyr with whom another woman would surely sympathize.

Instead, I was pierced by Bacall's angry green eyes. "You ass!" she said. "Now let me say something: You are making the biggest mistake of your life. You think a fella like Art comes along twice in a lifetime? Bogey and I have watched you two together for over a year, good times, rotten times, and you're perfect for each other. Furthermore, you may not know it yet because Art *is* young and roly-poly and a funny man about life, but he's the best guy you'll ever meet, kid!"

I looked at her in amazement. Then I brushed the tears from my eyes as Bogey and Art approached the booth. Silently I made my way through an enormous dinner ordered to make up for what Bogie cursed as "all those goddamned canned peas in Africa; only thing I could keep down." And I remained silent as we went first to a nightclub, then to a new bar we loved, Lisa's Water Gypsy, a houseboat on the Seine run by a Cincinnati girl who moved it to a new location every week. The French would not give her a license because they had no classification for a "floating 'boîte.' " We kept a taxi waiting while the four of us trundled from bridge to bridge hollering down into the darkness until finally Lisa's voice drifted up from under the pont Alexandre, "We're under here this week!"

Throughout the long evening my mind remained on Art, on all the wonderful things he meant to me. Betty's last words to me were a whispered warning; "Don't you dare take that job!"

Back in Art's room and lying in his arms, I confessed what I had done. Then I repeated what Betty had said and burst into tears. We both lay there weeping until Art said angrily, "Listen, if you want a job in New York, I can find you a better one than working in some cockamamie buying office. I have plenty of friends there who would be glad to help you."

This sent me into a fresh burst of tears. Art was actually offering to help me leave. We finally fell asleep in each other's arms, Art murmuring, "That would have been the dumbest thing you could have done." At dawn I crept back into my room as the maid clanked up the stairs with her brooms and pails.

The following day as I was leaving for the office, Art came in to ask if I'd wired New York to refuse the job. I said I had and that the man who hired me was furious.

"What a terrible thing to do, Miss McGarry," he had shouted. "We have already announced your arrival in *Women's Wear*."

ART: **Every time I see Betty Bacall I say to her, "Why didn't you mind your own damn business in Paris?"**

She breaks out laughing and says something like, "Listen, buster. It was the best thing anyone did for you."

I guess the truth of the matter was that had Ann done what she planned without telling me, she would have resolved my dilemma for me. Now it was back in my court and I didn't really want to deal with it. There was a part of me that wanted to be free and another part which made me fearful that if Ann left I would be alone

and never find anyone like her again. The indecision was driving me up the wall.

To stall for time, Art came up with a zany idea that would keep me in Paris. He suggested that I leave Balmain and open my own publicity office. I could service U.S. manufacturers who wanted their companies and products publicized in the French Couture. It sounded crazy to me. No one had tried such a thing before; besides, I had no capital. But Art's brainstorm was perfectly timed. During the preceding six months at Balmain, three different manufacturers had offered me money to publicize their products with Balmain's. In every case I had refused, but now the idea of doing it legally for my own firm appealed to me.

Art left me to think about it and set out for a week in Morocco, extracting my promise that I would not vanish before he returned.

I don't know what happened in Africa but when Art came back he had made up his mind. He pounded on my door, hollering from the hallway, "It's time you were up anyway. I've decided the only answer to our mess is to get married, so will you marry me?" I opened my door and we fell into each other's arms.

We were going to get married. We even came to a compromise on our different religions. Art promised that our children would be baptized and brought up as Catholics; and I gave my word that I would never blow up when Art expounded about how conservative and backward Catholics are, especially concerning politics. As part of my bargain, I also promised that our children would go to public, not Catholic, schools since Art seemed convinced that a six-year-old child could easily return from his first day at parochial school with a tiny white collar turned backwards around his neck.

With the question of marriage finally resolved (but not the date or even the year when we'd go through with it), Art happily renewed his plans for me to open my own publicity office in Paris. I'm sure he was stalling for time; setting up a new business was bound to take months or years.

"I'll invest in your company and perhaps Jim Nolan will; Maggie would make a terrific partner." Jim was by then head of Public Relations at TWA and was married to Maggie (née Claughton), who had stopped working as a journalist when their first baby was born.

Before proceeding further I went to see David Schoenbrun of CBS. I had known David even longer than Art and trusted his advice. We met that very afternoon and I asked him what he thought of Art's idea. Would it work? What were my chances?

"Annie," he said, "you're not asking me if I think an American should open a Paris publicity office—you're asking me if I think a Catholic can marry a Jew. The answer to both is YES." Then he added, "I'll go so far as to invest in your business myself if you'll include my wife Dorothy; she's a fabulous artist."

Maggie and I accepted, never dreaming it would be Dorothy who would make our business succeed financially as well as artistically.

After two months of searching, Maggie found a decrepit office for rent on avenue Président Wilson and Dorothy designed our letterhead: ANN MCGARRY ASSOCIATES. The reason my name appeared alone on the letterhead was that of the three partners I was the only one who had worked in a Paris publicity office. Maggie and Dorothy worked under their maiden names so if we flopped it wouldn't hurt their husbands' reputations.

We started with $1,500—five hundred dollars from each of the three men: Schoenbrun, Nolan, and Buchwald, two husbands and one lover.

We opened our business with one account, the Celanese Corporation of America, which paid us a monthly fee of $500 plus all expenses including unlimited travel on their behalf. We were hired by Norma Geer, who had once offered me a job as her assistant while I was still at Balmain. She was a top Celanese executive who had moved from New York to Paris with a three-fold plan: first, to introduce Celanese Acetate to the French fashion industry. Second, to infiltrate couture houses in London, Ireland, Italy, and Spain with Acetate satins, brocades, peau de soies, and velvets manufactured by leading local mills. Third, to open a French factory to manufacture Acetate fibers for the demand she would have created.

Norma took over an elegant suite at the exclusive Lancaster Hotel on the rue de Berri, renting it by the year as home and office. Because I had meetings with her almost every morning, she became my friend and in many ways a godmother to both Art and me. It was Norma who gave me a bridal shower, a bizarre idea to the French. But once they were reassured that it had nothing to do with bathing or weather, they went overboard and surprised me with an instant trousseau: Dior nightgowns, chiffon negligees, a maribou-trimmed kimono, and sexy black panties and garter belts.

Our office did such a thorough job for Celanese that by the end of six months leading Paris designers were using Acetate fabrics in their collections. Our successful campaign brought us other American clients: the Lace Industry, the Leather Industry, the Belt Association, a manufacturer of dazzling colored lizard skins—all wanting a Paris fashion connection. Robert Hall Clothes hired us to find them a French couturier who would design models which Robert Hall could copy at mass market prices.

ART: **There was no doubt the three American women were needed in Paris and their business would be a success.**

American companies were desperate for people who knew the American market, and Dorothy, Maggie, and Ann, each in her own way was very talented and skillful about the business. To my knowledge the only two American firms dealing in American clients who wanted publicity in the United States were Ann's publicity office and J. Walter Thompson. If you couldn't afford J. Walter Thompson you had to go to Ann, Dorothy, and Maggie. I don't think the three girls sent any business to J. Walter Thompson but the big agency sent many small accounts to the girls. David, Jim and I were

happy that they were happy. It gave us an opportunity to do our own thing without worrying about them getting bored.

There were quite a few bored American wives in Paris whose husbands either worked for the government, private companies, or were married to military personnel. They never took advantage of what Paris had to offer—griped incessantly about the French, were very unhappy because their husbands were constantly flying off to Italy, Switzerland, or some other place for their companies. Life was good, servants were plentiful, but they didn't know what to do with themselves. Many wound up having affairs, and a high percentage of marriages landed on the rocks.

I guess one of the big problems is that the French were difficult about allowing Americans to work (you needed a work permit) and the language barrier was too much for most of them.

The military wives had other problems. Some, not all, hated the waiting around. This was particularly true of Navy wives. I once went to Villefranche, in the south of France, where the Sixth Fleet wives were stationed, and did a story on them. Some loved the Riviera and were having a great old time. Others would have rather been in Norfolk, Virginia.

They never knew when their husbands would be coming back. The only clue they had, although security was tight, was when the French hookers started arriving in town. Somehow the girls always knew a week in advance when the fleet would be in. Unlike most American women, the Navy wives were happy as could be when the hookers showed up because that meant their husbands were coming home.

As our publicity firm grew, we moved outside the fashion industry. We secured French chefs' endorsements for Accent and arbitrarily injected monosodium glutamate into recipes served at three-star restaurants. We were hired by ASTA when 2,000 international travel agents surged into Paris for their convention. We even did a stint for the Swiss Watch Makers; Dorothy came up with creative props and I went to Switzerland to eat sauerkraut and mashed potatoes for an entire week.

We worked for 20th Century–Fox Films under the supervision of Sterling Silliphant who had come to Europe to publicize Fox's million-dollar film *David and Bathsheba* and twisted arms until several couturiers used a Biblical theme in their collections.

ART: **Surely you all remember the "David and Bathsheba" look? There was a tie-in with bath oil too!**

We also worked for Richard Condon at United Artists, whose wild, ingenious, and hilarious ideas made him the best in the movie business. If what he did was publicity, then we were running a Christian Science Reading Room.

We even snagged a few Paris accounts our first year, breaking down the resistance of the owner of the Hôtel George V, the Plaza Athenée, and the Tremoille and getting a contract to do publicity for all three. Monsieur Duprê resented paying for our services—he couldn't equate public realtions with "work"—but he swelled with pride when we handed him clippings from U.S. newspapers in which local travelers extolled his hotels.

Our husbands—silent, or occasionally vociferous, partners—were immensely helpful. Art gave us clever ideas and advance news for press releases. And David Schoenbrun had no compunction about recommending that our office publicize major CBS events as well as Paris appearances of their network stars, including Art Linkletter who, with his wife Lois, took Paris by storm. He knew intuitively so much about publicity that he did more for our reputation than we did for his CBS projects.

One assignment, however, was almost too much for us. David persuaded CBS and Smith Kline and French, a major pharmaceutical firm in Philadelphia, to hire us to publicize a live, closed-circuit television presentation of an appendectomy operation performed in living color at the Boucicaut Hospital in Paris.

Dr. Peter Goldmark, the genius who had invented color television and perfected the CBS system, headed a group of executives who flew to Paris to sell CBS's color system to government-owned French television.

Our office worked wonders until we came to the demonstration itself. At our first sight of real surgery, Dorothy and I dashed to the street, our hands over our mouths. Our secretary mercifully fainted in her seat. Despite our lack of follow-through, we received our full fee. We used a big chunk of it to take the whole gang on a farewell spree, ending the evening in a naughty cabaret where there was plenty of living color.

Despite our efforts, the CBS system was soon found to be incompatible with French television and France went on to develop its own color system, which is considered amongst the best in the world. We'll never know whether we—or someone with a sick appendix—helped them get started.

One of the most valuable people who worked with us was Betty Coffin, who wandered into our office during our first weeks in business, assured us she would work for peanuts, and stayed with us to the end, enthusiastically taking on all our fashion photography at a weekly salary of $30. She actually outlasted our company. When Dorothy and I eventually decided to disband, Bettina—a name she was immediately christened by the French press—was retained by two of our clients on a free-lance basis. They could find no one as good.

Bettina had arrived in Paris without a place to live or to unpack two steamer trunks of clothes amassed during her days at *Vogue*. So she stored them in a musty closet in the hallway outside our office. I can still see her tossing clouds of petticoats, chiffon blouses, stockings, underwear, and scarves into the air, mumbling frantically, "I know there's a pair of pink satin pumps in here." Ten minutes later she would be dressed like a *Vogue* model, ready for a big evening.

Bettina was an expert at setting up fashion photographs. Eventually she knew every model in France, England, and Italy plus the Americans who were trying to hit big-time during the Paris openings.

I envied Bettina's tall, reed-thin figure and her shining straight platinum hair. "My natural color? Are you mad, girl? I have no idea what it would be if I ever stopped sloshing it with a couple bottles of peroxide every three weeks."

Bettina was always broke because she couldn't resist sale-priced luxuries in the Couture. One day she appeared in a dramatic black and white ponyskin coat, the hit of Schiaparelli's collection, reduced from several thousand dollars to $500. "So they'll just have to wait for my rent, that's all there is to it," she responded when Dorothy and I asked how in the world she had paid for the knockout.

Her mother and father despaired of ever seeing her again, so they sent her a round-trip ticket to New York. However, Bettina had no money for auxiliary expenses such as airline charges for overweight luggage—we were limited to forty pounds, considered featherweight by most women and duty for French imports. Bettina solved the problem by removing all labels and then wearing everything she needed for a two-week stay. On her way to the airport she made her taxi wait while she ran into our apartment to show Art and me how she'd managed. She looked like a blimp. She was wearing two skirts, two blouses, one sweater, one silk dress, a wool suit, an overcoat, and a raincoat. She lamented, "I can't even raise my arms to hug you goodbye; do you think Customs will notice?" On her return she bragged about not having to pay a penny—the Customs official took one look at the poor fat lady and didn't even ask her to open the small suitcase she was carrying.

There was no possibility of obtaining a work permit for Bettina. We paid her under the table, listing her salary as postage one week, taxis the next, whatever would arouse the least suspicion. Toward the end of her first year with our office, an inspector visited us, fortunately while she was out at a shooting. "I see a beautiful blonde mademoiselle in this office every time I inspect it, yet there is no record of her having a work permit!"

Dorothy thought fast. "But monsieur, surely you must realize that the beautiful blonde works merely for pleasure. She has no need of money. She has many gentlemen friends who supply all her needs." The inspector smiled with understanding and never bothered us again about Bettina, who continued working without a permit until she got married.

Our business was booming when seventeen months after we opened we were suddenly given an eviction notice. The government was returning our old building to the estate of its original owner. They had confiscated it right after the war, claiming that he had collaborated with the Germans, but now had changed their minds.

The eviction notice arrived the week I was leaving for London to get married, but fortunately Dorothy had blossomed into a business whiz. While Art and I were honeymooning, she scoured Paris until she found an office we could afford to buy, not rent, and even more astoundingly, one on the Champs-Élysées, the most respected commercial location in Paris. She withdrew every cent from our bank account and bought the lease. By the time I returned our lease was registered by the French government. We were landlords!

There was just one problem. We had never formally registered our business, claiming it as a small cottage industry. Soon after we bought our new office the French Finance Department informed us in foreboding phrases that we would be imprisoned if we continued to conduct business without a license.

We could no longer plead that our company was a one-woman venture, yet we knew that as Americans we would never be granted a legal French business license. We had gotten by so far only because the French regarded our work as a joke.

David Schoenbrun came to our rescue once again by divulging the only way out—bribery. "Annie, you'll have to do it yourself in a way that allows the French to save face. Just tell them all the regulations confused you."

David arranged my illicit meeting with a finance official at Chez Alexandre's, an outdoor café on the Champs-Élysées where we would look like two friends having apéritifs. With shaky nonchalance, I walked toward a specified table at the appointed hour. I checked my purse—the bulging envelope was on top where I could grab it. My hands were trembling as I glanced across the street where Art and David sat at a small table at Fouquet's, silently cheering me on. Within moments, a stranger approached my table, picking me out of the crowded terrace from David's description of what I'd be wearing. He was as relaxed as a lazy cat, but I was so tense I waited only until he'd been served to blurt out my memorized speech. As instructed, I then reached under the table as if to pick up something and, exactly as David had predicted, found the man's arm already there, his hand open to accept the envelope. Neither of us said another word; the official left without finishing his drink. I dashed recklessly across avenue George V to Art and David who were laughing and clapping. Our license arrived by messenger the following day, and Dorothy rushed it off to be added to our new letterhead.

ART: **Bribery was a way of life in France. The French bureaucracy thrived on it. I've always been a coward about bribing someone because I'm sure I'll get caught. This day was one of the most uncomfortable of my life. I had visions of calling up Ann's mother and saying, "I don't know how to tell you this but your daughter is in the Santé prison." I was also selfish about it and saw my whole career going down the drain for some stupid publicity business that we had put our women in to keep them from bugging us.**

When the transaction was made and license deliv-

ered I was perspiring all over. I expected the gendarmes to say, "Monsieur will you kindly step into the black maria?"

I may have been laughing and clapping, but I was also shaking. Making someone legal by doing something illegal is not my idea of having a good time in Paris.

One day not long after our move to the Champs Élysées we were hired by Ed Gottlieb, head of his own successful New York public relations firm which handled the entire French Cognac industry. Our contract stipulated that we would work closely with an American account executive named Henry McNulty, who was living in London.

While we were still researching the unique history and quality of French Cognac, Henry McNulty telephoned from the airport saying he'd flown over to meet us and to start work on some new ideas.

From the moment Henry walked into our office—fair-haired and dashingly handsome, dressed to perfection in an English camel's-hair coat—I noticed that Bettina sat silently at her desk, doodling on the back of her hand, contributing nothing to our session.

At the close of the meeting, when Henry left the room, Bettina yelped, "I've fallen in love! That is the man I want to marry. And don't tell me he's already married or something, it doesn't matter—someday, somehow I am going to M-A-R-R-Y him!" And she did, one year later, when Henry and his wife completed divorce proceedings that they had begun before he moved abroad. He and Bettina are still blissfully happy, with a grown daughter named Claudia. When Bettina talks about Henry her voice is as full of wonder as the day she first saw him.

In the fall of 1953, when Art and I had been married for a year, our publicity office got a lucky break, but in the end it forced both Dorothy and me to take a hard look at our lives. Maggie had left the business when her second daughter was born, so Dorothy and I, even with Bettina's help, were working double-time. We vaguely recalled giving an interview to *Fortune's* Paris correspondent one rainy afternoon several months earlier. At the time we assumed the reporter was merely trying to show his New York office that he was working. We were completely surprised when his article ran, under the heading TWO AMERICAN GIRLS IN PARIS. It began: "Starting a business in Paris and grossing $40,000 in the second year is equal to grossing $400,000 in the same time in the United States." It went on: "If the proprietors are women, it's an even better record—for women, while highly thought of in France, are thought of not at all as businesswomen." The article listed our clients and the work we were doing, winding up with, "They have a degree of economic independence enjoyed by few wives in France. Dorothy Scher is married to David Schoenbrun, head of CBS in Paris; Ann McGarry is married to the *New York Herald Tribune*'s Art Buchwald, who writes the column, 'Europe's Lighter Side.' Their expenses—a modest office on the Champs-Élysées, a French secretary, and a fashion assistant—are a small part of their 14-million-franc gross. What's left over is enough in francs to add up importantly in dollars."

Dorothy and I shrieked as we read the article. Forty thousand dollars? We had exaggerated for the reporter, never dreaming the figure would appear in print.

During the weeks following the *Fortune* article, we began receiving letters of inquiry from impressively large American firms—a tire company, an oil conglomerate, an international marketing firm, a leading distiller, each requesting a presentation. What publicity program could we create for them and when could they expect to receive a detailed proposal? One company hedged its interest in our firm by stipulating that they would accept only a male account executive for any program emanating from our office.

Dorothy and I realized we were in deep trouble. "Male account executive" meant hiring an experienced American at a New York-scale salary, and moving him to Paris to work for us. As the letters piled up we knew we were at a crossroads; we had to go one of two ways. Enlarge our office, import a couple of high-powered men from the States, go after bigger accounts at higher fees, and devote every waking hour to making a profit.

Or we could quit.

After more than three years of total service to our clients, Dorothy and I had grown weary of juggling the demands of business and family. We were consistenly arriving home only seconds before our guests arrived for cocktails or dinner. David Schoenbrun grew increasingly angry every time he was forced to summon Dorothy home from the office. As tensions grew, Dorothy and I made a pact: "Whenever a male voice calls for either of us after six P.M., say 'She just left for home.' " One evening around 7:15 David called and I delivered the pat lie. He exploded. "Don't give me that crap, Annie, put Dorothy on the phone. I know she's there, and this is an emergency." We dissolved the pact, because the emergency that night was the early arrival of the then ignored Charles de Gaulle for dinner.

Until the *Fortune* article appeared, neither Dorothy nor I had the nerve to confess we wanted to stop working. I was certain I would be hurting Dotty or at least letting her down. Art said, "Be honest: the *Fortune* article has changed everything. Either you go big-time or you stop while you're ahead. Dorothy will understand and agree."

The following Monday morning I stopped in the ladies' room outside our office to rehearse once more what I planned to say to Dorothy. Someone was in the cubicle next to mine. It was Dorothy, rehearsing what she was going to say to me. Like Music Hall Rockettes we stepped out in unison, and as if by signal, blurted identical words: "LET'S GET OUT!" So much for fancy prepared speeches.

We went into our office, divided the letters we'd received following the *Fortune* article, and sent the same answer to every company who'd contacted us:

> Thank you for your interest in our publicity firm which we are terminating at the end of this month. We have decided to

With Pierre Balmain, who hired me to do his public relations in 1949 despite the fact I spoke no French.

The clothes were great—
the salary was nothing.

Above, left, Art in Paris in 1948. *Right*, with Danny Kaye and his wife, Sylvia, in Paris *Herald* offices. He always took VIPs there after dinner as part of the tour. *Below*, Art, myself, Skitch Henderson and Faye Emerson, who came to Paris on their honeymoon. Faye was the hottest star in television at the time and was "hot" news.

Above, Charlie MacArthur, the writer; Mary Martin; Art; Helen Hayes; George Abbott; Jamie MacArthur; and Richard Halliday. Mary, Helen, and George had come to Paris to do Thornton Wilder's *The Skin of Our Teeth*, while Charlie played with Art. *Below, left*, sightseeing with Anita Loos and Helen Hayes. *Right*, at the Longchamps race course with Betty Bacall and Humphrey Bogart.

Above, 24 rue Boccador. The top floor is where Art and I lived in separate rooms—connected by the very convenient balcony. *Left*, Art and I at the flea market, where he bought all his hats. Once he found a French marshal's hat, which we put in the foyer of our apartment and frightened everyone who came in.

Left, a passport picture is a passport picture is a passport picture. *Below*, the coat is by Balmain, the cobblestones are real, and Gene Kelly just danced by with Leslie Caron.

Left, our wedding day in London in the doorway of Westminster Cathedral. It took me two years to get Art to pose for this picture. *Below*, cutting the cake. The girls belong to harmonica player Larry Adler and Gene and Betsy Kelly. Perle Mesta stayed over for the wedding, and Norma Geer (far right) gave us the party at Claridge's. Fred Tupper, who worked for Pan American Airways, gave Art away.

Right, the honeymoon in Majorca at Formentor. Art played Ping-Pong most of the time. *Below*, I don't know why we posed for this picture, but it must have been a happy occasion.

JOE COVELLO

Art seemed to be always on the road looking for columns. *Above, right*, with Greg Peck at St. Moritz. *Left*, then in the Congo writing a piece for *Collier's*. *Below*, then off to Marrakesh. I stayed home to watch the French government and the children. (JOE COVELLO)

Above, Elizabeth Taylor, Connie, and Joel at the Hôtel Meurice in Paris. *Below, left*, Mary Martin, Connie, and Jennifer at Fouquet's on a Sunday morning. *Right*, Lucille Ball with her brood and ours in front of the Hôtel George V.

Happy days in the Parc Monceau apartment with Jenny, Connie, and Joel. (MARK SHAW)

Above, a scene from *Person to Person* with Charles Collingwood. The children stole the show, and everyone who saw it in the States thought we had it made—which we did. *Below*, Joel and Jennifer go to town on the food during the program. It was taped at four o'clock and we hadn't fed them all day.

I did get to travel with Art once in a while. *Left*, behind us is Greece. *Below, left*, the Sphinx. On my right is my camel driver. We usually wound up at these exotic places because Conrad Hilton was always opening a new hotel somewhere and we went along on the junket.

There were lots of American movies being made in Europe at the time. *Above, left*, we are in Avila for the shooting of *The Pride and the Passion*, and on the right in Rome with Eddie Fisher on the set of *Cleopatra*. If Richard Burton was having a thing with Elizabeth, we were the last three people to know it. *Below*, Art and I at the opening of the Vienna State Opera—an historic event that compelled him to wear his first white tie.

Above, Horace Sutton, the travel writer, tries to throw Art into the Trevi Fountain because he claimed if he did he would get his wish. *Right*, this photo was taken by Doug Kirkland for *Look*. Art was dancing in front of the Eiffel Tower at the time.

Above, Henry Fonda, Darryl Zanuck and Edmund O'Brien at a French café during a break in the shooting of *The Longest Day*. *Below*, Paul Newman, Duke Ellington, and Art on the set of *Paris Blues*. (SAM SHAW)

SAM SHAW

It's 1962 and we're homeward bound on the *Queen Mary*. The moveable feast from now on will only be a memory for us all.

become wives and mothers again, and are switching from public to domestic relations to take care of our husbands, children, friends, and homes. Sincerely. . . .

Within two hours we'd mailed the letters, packed up our files, and called our lawyer requesting that he sell our lease for the best price he could get. For the first time in years we got home before our husbands.

Four

Art and I had obstinately refused to believe we couldn't be married in Paris. It was our town, the city that had brought us together. Grateful and romantic, I wanted to be wed there. Besides, it was the only place where we could afford to get married.

"It'll be a mess, wait and see," our good friend Charles Torem warned us. He was the best young American lawyer in Paris, brilliant and handsome, the rising star of Coudert Frères, an international law firm.

When Art and I insisted on trying to bulldoze our way through the French bureaucracy Charlie offered to prepare our myriad legal documents as a wedding present. Days passed before he summoned us to his office and handed over a mountain of papers to be signed and countersigned; it took an hour. I scrawled my full name on the final page: Ann Marie Mercedes McGarry (for my Confirmation name I'd chosed Mercedes in honor of a poet I'd discovered that year). "Done!" I smiled as Art nudged me and said mischievously, "One small codicil, please; in this bottom space write in twenty-five words or less: 'I, Ann McGarry, want to marry Art Buchwald because. . . .' I want it on record," he explained to Charlie, who grabbed the page before I messed up his legal handiwork.

How I envied my sister Joannie who was planning her own wedding helped by my mother and a parish priest who automatically furnished the few needed documents. "You're having it easy, girlie, getting married in Warren," I wrote her, "but if we break through this Paris red tape I'll be twice as married as you!"

French law dictated that a couple planning a religious wedding be married twice, the first time in a civil ceremony by the mayor of the quarter where the couple resided. Only after the mayor's records had been processed were they free to go to a church for the real thing.

We didn't get that far. But we tried our best for three frustrating days. Every morning at eight o'clock, carrying Charlie's fat manila envelope, we plunged into a taxi and headed across the Seine to scurry from one municipal office to another, begging uniformed officials for directions, queuing up in lines of fifty or sixty applicants, slowly edging up to a window only to be turned away because we were in the wrong line. It was a nightmare. No one smiled at us or winked or wished us luck. Instead, clerks barked harshly, one actually cackling with delight as he turned us down, as if to say: Ha! trapped two more stupid Americans.

At noon we'd take a lunch break at a nearby café where we slipped off our shoes, reviving our feet. By the end of the third day we were convinced we'd beaten the system. We pushed our crumpled papers through a final window to the man who issued the marriage permit. After examining them carefully, he said, "Everything seems to be in order except for Mademoiselle's *carte de sêjour*. She is a temporary resident so there will be a delay of fifteen days."

The bureaucracy had won again; we left empty-handed, so dispirited we couldn't imagine starting all over again in fifteen days. As we limped out of the old building, Art muttered, "I'll say this for France, it sure gives a guy time to change his mind about marriage."

* * *

ART: **I don't wish to sound like a rat but I wasn't as discouraged about the French bureaucracy as Ann was. I guess deep down I was counting on it. For one thing I still wasn't sure I wanted to get married. At the same time I didn't want to be the heavy if we didn't. The Napoleonic Code has saved many a foreign man (and probably woman) by its red tape.**

There was an American sportswriter on the Paris *Herald* who used to propose to every girl he went out with counting on some nasty French official to throw him out because he didn't have the right papers.

This went on for several years, with various women, until one day he found someone in the French marriage license bureau who was a romantic, and okayed everything although the sportswriter's papers were not in order.

The poor newspaperman was dumbfounded and the next thing he knew he was saying "I do" and the last I heard is now somewhere in Iowa trying to support a large family.

I, of course, cursed the French bureaucracy with Ann and put on a show of indignation which could have won me an Academy Award if it had been filmed. I don't recall saying "It sure gives a guy time to change his mind." Rather, I'm sure I said something like "It's a Goddamn tragedy when two people in love are thwarted by French red tape when trying to find the happiness they so richly deserve."

That night, hoping to cheer me up, Art invited Lena Horne, her husband Lennie Hayton, and her little girl Gail to join us at an out-of-the-way restaurant famous for its soups. When Lena asked why we seemed so depressed, we described our frustration and she told us about a wedding she'd been to in London last month and the wonderful Jesuit priest she had met. He was a saint, she said, and known for helping displaced Americans work out their marriage arrangements. All either of us had to do was establish a two-week residency in London.

ART: **What choice did I have? I will say I hold no bitterness towards Lena Horne to this day. She was just trying to be helpful, and it wasn't her fault she knew an accommodating priest in London.**

After dinner we drifted home on a pink cloud. No more red tape, no more lines, no more papers to fill out. Art decided to go to London immediately to talk to the Jesuit and see if he could get me a dispensation to marry a non-Catholic and stay within the church.

My last thought as I fell asleep was that now I would not need a French-English dictionary to understand my wedding. I was always nervous that the French ceremony added to "love, cherish and obey" a few words about doing the marketing twice daily for fresh bread.

My euphoria vanished twenty-four hours later when Art called from London. "I met Father Mills. He's a whiz, but he can't do a damn thing about your dispensation. He says only the Cardinal can waive restrictions and he is out of the country for two months. Mills says not to give up, though. I'll come back on the night ferry."

ART: **Here again my memory of my meeting with Mills varies with that of Ann's. As I recall the conversation with him it went like this.**

"Father, I wish to marry an American Catholic girl."

"That's perfectly all right," he said.

"But I'm not Catholic."

"What are you?"

> **"Jewish," I said.**
> **"Thank God," he said. "I was afraid you were a Protestant."**
> **It may have been true that the Cardinal had to give his blessing, but I was in such a daze I'll have to take Ann's word for it.**

Maybe it was psychosomatic but after Art's call I came down with a virulent case of flu. When Art returned he found me in bed with swollen eyes, greasy hair and a complexion that flashed like a traffic light from bilious yellow to blinding red. "Are you sure you want to go through with it?" I whispered. Art laughed to cover his shock, told me to try to sleep, and returned an hour later with a sandwich two feet long and leaking obscenely from every side with cold cuts, tomatoes, mustard, and cheese. "Eat it," he ordered. "It'll give you strength." Oddly enough it did.

The next night I secretly took a cab to St.-Joseph's, the only American church in Paris. I rarely went there for Mass since there were so many French churches closer by. I didn't even know the pastor's name when I asked for an audience. I was directed to the Rectory where I lined up in the anteroom alongside eight or ten other people waiting their turns to get into the pastor's private office. It was so quiet that I could hear everything being said inside. A couple from SHAPE headquarters was turned down flat when they asked for a dispensation because one of them was a Baptist, so when my turn came I was steeled for the pastor's angry edict: "It can't be done overnight, you know. Don't think this is like buying a new dress, young lady." Then, leaning over his desk, he shouted, "AND in addition, the man (at least he didn't say 'your pagan lover') will have to take at least six lessons of instruction in Catholicism. We could try to work them in . . . say, two a week . . . if the assistant pastors aren't too busy." Finally, bobbing his head toward the ceiling in search of spiritual strength, he lamented, "Why is everybody suddenly demanding dispensations? The church doesn't approve at all, you know. Well, come back next week, you can see how busy I am, much too busy, who's next out there?"

As I left his office I heard him start bawling out a new petitioner and I realized that regardless of the request his answers would be NO.

Out of habit I went to early Mass the next morning at St.-Pierre-de-Chaillot, a majestic cathedral just two blocks away from my room. I'd been going there on and off for almost two years but had never felt totally comfortable because the building was so cold and modern with stark gray concrete walls and bare altars. That day there were only a handful of penitents, all women, kneeling on high-backed wicker chairs, which each had tugged to a favorite location at the foot of the altar. No French church had permanently fixed pews.

When Mass was over, almost without thinking, I tiptoed over to a tall, handsome young priest, pulled his sleeve, and whispered that it was imperative I talk to him about a dispensation to marry a non-Catholic. My French poured out in miraculously perfect phrases. Words I couldn't remember learning came to the tip of my tongue. Instead of brushing me aside, or asking me to make an appointment, he sat down beside me on one of the rickety chairs, and we talked for an hour. It was only later that I learned he was the premier vicaire of St.-Pierre-de-Chaillot, addressed as Monsieur l'Abbé Cappelle. I called him Father throughout our discussion but he didn't seem to mind. He looked like a professional football player. His eyes twinkled with humor and genuine curiosity. It turned out that his younger brother was studying journalism and Father Cappelle had been translating Art's columns for over a year. He was one of Art's fans.

ART: **This was one fan I didn't need.**

Toward the end of our conversation, I had a momentary scare as he began recounting the heavy responsibilities of a mixed-faith marriage. He warned me about what, as a Catholic, I would be required to do, how I'd be expected to conduct my life and told me that I would have to pray constantly for Art's conversion. Just when I was certain he was planning to turn me down, he slapped his big hands on his knees, stood up, and said, "Eh bien, tell Monsieur Buchwald to come see me tomorrow night at seven. We'll figure out how to arrange everything."

Fortunately Art and Father Cappelle got along famously, agreeing on almost everything—football, politics, the French government, the President of the United States, soccer, Communism. In fact, when Art described the meeting I wondered if religion was even touched upon until Art added, "Oh, he made *me* agree to one thing: that our children will be Catholics all the way."

I swallowed and waited a few seconds, almost scared to ask, "Will that be difficult for you?"

"Difficult?" said Art. "Not at all; you're the one who has to do all the work. All I have to do is promise, and I promised."

Through the years Art more than kept his promise. Even before we had children, wherever we traveled, after signing the hotel register, Art would always ask, "Where's the nearest Catholic church and what time are the Masses on Sunday?"

The final step in obtaining the dispensation I had to take by myself. Gathering up courage, I went over to the Left Bank offices of the Archbishop of Paris. A frail old priest greeted me, examined the papers Father Cappelle had prepared, and, noting the date we had set for the wedding was October 11, less than three weeks away, he said, "Well, there isn't time for this to go to Rome—I assume the premier vicaire realizes that—so we'll have to send your documents directly to London. Unfortunately that will cost 500 francs. If you don't have the money I'll wait while you go home to get it." I handed him five 100 franc notes (totalling about $1) and he began scratching information from my original papers into an ancient black album. It was three Bibles thick and so old I would not have been surprised to find *Arc, Joan of* on the first page. Then he affixed the red seal of the Archbishop of Paris, shook my hand, and padded behind me as I walked out of the quiet, book-lined room with the parchment dispensation clutched in my hand.

With our wedding plans finally underway and Art leaving to establish his two-week residency in London, it was time to think about a wedding dress. I ended up getting two! The first was for my own wedding and wasn't a dress at all, but an elegant coat and skirt ensemble which Balmain offered to design as a wedding gift. The second was the real thing—traditional white satin with a train—but it was for my younger sister Joannie whose wedding was to take place one month after ours, and who had written, "There isn't a single gown in or around Warren that I haven't seen on at least six brides this past year. Can you send me something wonderful from one of the Paris stores?"

I didn't have the heart to tell her that all Paris brides, rich or poor, had their wedding dresses made from scratch, even if they had to whip them up themselves, and that French department stores didn't have bridal departments. Instead I told her that Art and I would have her dress made in Paris as her wedding gift. "All you have to do is okay the enclosed design."

During the following two weeks I would hurry first to Balmain's where I'd stand for a fitting of my own outfit, then take the Métro out to the suburbs and try on Joannie's dress which was being made by Mademoiselle Perrère, an unknown but expert young dressmaker who could copy anything. Because my sister was so much smaller and shorter, the hardest part of the project was convincing the dressmaker to baste the dress so that it fit me perfectly, then to reduce all measurements to those of the actual bride.

When the dress was finished, we ran into friends from Warren who'd been visiting Paris and who eagerly agreed to smuggle the voluminous bridal gown into the United States. Joannie wrote ecstatically that her dress fit to perfection even to the six-buttoned long tight sleeves.

* * *

ART: While Ann was having all these clothes made I was in London sitting out the two weeks residency. It was a long time to think about what I was getting into.

Before the females who read this book get too angry at me let me explain what was going on in my mind. I was not familiar with marriage and scared stiff of the responsibilities that went with it. I never knew my mother and had been raised in a series of foster homes. At an early age I had become a loner. The people who played the strongest roles in my life were my foster mothers and my three sisters. I had no brothers. I saw my father every weekend, but since I wasn't living with him, I hadn't figured out that relationship. So I was really frightened of women, and frightened of getting permanently attached to one, since I was used to the impermanence of being shuffled around to different homes.

I didn't take getting married lightly. While I saw all sorts of things happening, I never said, "If it doesn't work I can always get out."

Then there was the responsibility of a wife and a family, which I wasn't sure I was up to dealing with. When the going got rough I always took off—first running away to join the U.S. Marine Corps, then going to USC and when that palled hopping a boat for Europe. I had been raised to just think of myself and take care of myself. The thought of answering, responding and being permanently involved with others scared the hell out of me.

Finally I thought about my career. How was I going to be a writer if I had to settle down?

A writer had to live—he had to travel and do things and have experiences. He had to work on banana boats and pick grapes and unload ships and ride the freight trains and fall in and out of love a dozen times and suffer! What would happen to the Great American Novel if I settled down in some apartment in Paris feeding milk bottles to babies?

My thoughts were noble in London. Was I doing the right thing by Ann? I knew I'd make a lousy husband. Wouldn't it be better if I told her now than if she found out for herself later?

I'm sure that these doubts are legitimate ones and all people have them. But my ways of dealing with them have been different from those of others. I used to retch in the bathroom. Years later when I went into analysis my psychiatrist and I figured out that it was my way of trying to say something. So there I was at the Ritz Hotel in London overlooking Hyde Park, gagging away in the bathroom at all hours of the night, while Ann was dreaming of me efficiently working out the plans for the big wedding day.

I had selected Fred Tupper, the public relations man for Pan American, to be my best man. John Huston and José Ferrer were making *Moulin Rouge* in London and they were delighted they had a wedding (someone else's) to look forward to. Gene Kelly said he wanted to come and two friends from our Paris days, Larry Adler, the harmonica player, and his lovely wife Eileen, insisted on giving us a pre-wedding party.

Al Hix, whom I worked with on USC's humor magazine, the *Wampus*, was in town and so were others. The wedding was picking up steam and was not going to be the quiet one Ann and I wanted.

I also had my problems with the English priest. I was pretty sore by this time that the Catholic hierachy had been such a pain in the ass about okaying our marriage. For one thing I felt I was giving up more than Ann was.

After all, they were getting everything their way. My father was pretty shaken by the idea I was marrying a Catholic girl, as was everyone else in my family.

Therefore, the more pressure they put on me the madder I got at the priest who had been assigned my case.

I recall one meeting in which I said, "Whatever I do I'm not going to kneel."

"Why?" he asked. "You've got a game leg, have you?"

So the two weeks were fraught with anxiety, gagging, fighting and nightmares. Even when Tupper took me to Simpson's Department Store on Piccadilly for my dark blue serge suit I was a shaken man.

I don't recall getting any sympathy from anyone. The idea that I was losing my freedom seemed to please all my friends. I thought to myself, Here I am on the top of the Tower of London and everyone is screaming for me to JUMP.

On the morning of October 10, with all papers in order, I was finishing my packing. In twenty-four hours I'd be a married woman. Norma Geer was trying to calm me by describing the details of the reception she had arranged at the Claridge's hotel in London. As we were folding my Balmain wedding outfit she gasped: "My God, what's wrong with your neck? You must be getting something, you're bright red!"

"It's from the mustard plaster," I wailed, lifting up my blouse to show her my back. When my flu had dragged on, settling in my chest, I'd obediently purchased what a French friend recommended as a sure cure: an old-time mustard plaster. Now Art was in for another shock—a barbecued bride.

Before leaving my room I wrote a letter, the last I'd write as a spinster, to my mother: "Aren't you glad I'm being married an ocean away? And that after tomorrow you'll have only Joannie's wedding to worry about? Of course if I had come home for mine you might have made the *Guinness Book of Records* for having two nervous breakdowns within thirty days."

I missed my mother most at that moment, but didn't want her to know it. We had never mentioned financing a trip to England for either her or Art's father. They were too proud. Still, I thought as I sat in my empty room, it would have been wonderful to charter a plane and fill it with everyone we loved. Then I dried my eyes and added a postscript. "Tell Gram we made Winchell's column. The *Herald Tribune*'s London bureau received a cable from New York yesterday: ASK BUCHWALD SEND STORY ON HIS WEDDING AND WHY DID WINCHELL SCOOP US."

On my wedding day I had breakfast with Norma in her room down the hall from mine at the Claridge's. She'd arrived in London Friday afternoon in time for a pre-wedding party Larry and Eileen Adler gave for us and to check final reception plans with Claridge's banquet manager.

After breakfast I calmly sat down to sew white lace on the slip I planned to wear for the ceremony. It was the only white one I had and very luxurious but five inches too long for my skirt, so I'd hacked it off in Paris and planned to add the lace hem in London. Why it was so important I'll never guess. Then I bathed, rolled up my hair, and tried to relax, but when my white bridal bouquet arrived shortly after noon I fell apart and couldn't even straighten my stocking seams. Still I insisted on dressing alone in my room. At 1:30 I was ready, my mother's rosary cutting holes in my tightly clenched fist. Norma by then was more jittery than I was and called me to her room for a glass of champagne before we left. Naomi Barry; my indispensable friend from Paris, arrived to comb my hair and gave me sixpence for my shoe, a blue garter, and something borrowed (a piece of Kleenex). Then I combed *her* hair. On our way to the church the three of us peeked into the reception room at the buffet table piled with English delicacies. The maître d'hotel poured three more glasses of champagne but after two sips I began hiccuping and put mine down. We climbed into the limousine Art had ordered and I held my breath all the way to Westminster Cathedral, determined to stop hiccuping before the ceremony.

We were to be married at a small side altar of the massive cathedral, the ceremony a brief one since the church disallowed a Mass unless both bride and groom were Catholic. We hadn't considered sending invitations; in fact Art had told our London friends to bypass the wedding at 3:00 P.M. and come directly to the reception—that's where the real action would be. But after all the delays, this was something they intended to see with their own eyes. Fifty familiar faces beamed at me as I entered the church. It was like a party, everybody smiling and waving, Sam Spiegel clasping his hands over his head like a champ after a long tough fight.

Art and Fred Tupper, his best man, stood in the doorway. Art looked so nervous and cute, his new tie matching Tup's (Tup had rushed out to buy them that morning after he inspected Art's wardrobe). Father Milne seemed the only calm person there. He led us to two chairs in front of the altar, prompting me, "Take off your other glove, Ann, for later." Norma quickly stepped up to grab my purse and fold back my three-button white kid, which stuck like glue. When Father Milne said, "Arthur, er, Art, er, Mr. Buchwald, take Ann's right hand," Art's was so cold that I had to hold it until it absorbed a little of my own warmth. But when Father Milne said to Art, "Now say on touching the thumb, 'In the name of the Father,' touching the first finger, 'and the Son,' touching the second finger, 'and the Holy Ghost' "—Art actually performed the ritual.

Later Norma said, "Did you realize what Art said?" I knew how hard it had been for him to do so. Years later he would shock me again at Ethel Kennedy's, saying, "Okay, if no one else will say Grace before dinner, I will." And he rattled off the entire prayer: "Bless us, O Lord, and these Thy gifts which we are about to receive from thy bounty in the name of the Father, Son, and Holy Spirit" in Hebrew.

After the ceremony we went to Caxton Hall, where Mr. Creagh, a civil servant said, "I have to marry you, too!" Another five minutes and we were bound together by Church and State. As Tup and Norma were signing as witnesses, Art asked, "What was that he threw at me?" and I said, "Holy water." Beaming with delight, Art said, "He ROONED my tie!" Then I put Art's ring on his finger. When he and Tup had gone to pick it up earlier that morning, it had been too small, so they had rushed to an area of wholesale jewelry stores where they found one wide enough for Art's finger. I think it is gold, but we never did check.

As we left the church, I reminded Art to kiss me and when we turned around there was Father Mills, Lena Horne's friend. "Congratulations, Mrs. Buchwald," he said and then yelled, "Art, we made it!" They slapped each other on the back as if they were celebrating a winning touchdown in the last seconds of a game. "You see," Father Mills said to Tup and Norma, "Art and I really had quite a time with all this blah, blah, blah," and I hoped that from then on Art would no longer fear priests.

Eighty people came to our reception including some of our friends' children. Larry and Eileen Adler had brought their two little girls, Carol and Wendy, and Gene Kelly and his wife Betsy had their cute little girl Kerry who screamed, "A charm for me, Ann, promise!" Later, I watched as the little kids and a waiter chopped into the cake looking for charms. Rather than mess up a three tiered confection, I promised the first charm to Kerry on their next visit to Paris.

Also at the reception were John Huston, José Ferrer, and Perle Mesta. One Jewish screenwriter walked up, lifted his glass of champagne, and said, "Mazeltov, as we say in our religion!" and Art said, "And God bless you, as we say in *ours*!"

Around 5:00 P.M. Tup said it was time to cut the cake—it was a delicious fruit and chocolate concoction with a butter-honey mixture under the white icing. Instead of a formal toast, Tup said that all of Art's friends had been trying to get us married for years. "We tried it in Luxembourg, in Paris, in Rome—and now it's not only perfect that it's happened in London, but it's also—ABOUT TIME!" Larry and Eileen gave us beautiful English silver candlesticks and on the card were the same words: "It's about time!"

ART: **Well, the deed was done and it was a nice wedding. The last thing I expected was to be married in Westminster Cathedral and have a reception at Claridge's, the poshest hotel in the Western world.**

I did enjoy myself and there were moments that I was having such a good time I forgot the wedding was mine.

Probably the best thing about it is we didn't have to deal with our respective families. There were none there. Had there been there would have been a lot of dirty looks, hurt feelings and very little high spirits. Mixed-faith marriages are more acceptable now than they were in 1952, and I honestly believe had the ceremony taken place in the U.S. without a rabbi in the room the turnout from my side of the family would have been very, very poor.

Our reception was over at 5:30 and Art and I went upstairs to what last night had been my room. Tup had secretly moved in all of Art's gear before the reception broke up. Overcome by a desire to be domestic, I let Art take the first shower while I began hanging up his clothes. I was so nervous and hot I stripped down to panties and bra, unaware that in English hotels the staff serving your room walk in and then tap gently on the door. Suddenly a stiff-upper-lipped butler in striped pants and waistcoat stood beside me with a cooler of champagne. I hadn't heard either his knock or his approaching feet. Completely unperturbed by my state of undress, he hurried to my side.

"Let me show you the proper way to hang trousers, madame, so they won't slip off the hanger as these will the way you are doing it." And he showed me: you lay out the trousers flat on the bed, pat them smooth, fold back one pant leg to exactly half its length, place the hanger at that spot, fold the cuff end up to the crotch, turn the trousers over, and do the same with the other pant leg—a hurricane couldn't blow it off the hanger and miraculously the wrinkles come out faster.

Although few couples get much sleep on their wedding night, they usually don't stay up to use the phone, but Art and I were awake until dawn trying to place a call to my mother. First the operators said, "Midnight, for sure." At midnight they said, "Two or three hours delay." At 5:00 A.M. we got another call from the operator announcing "a further six-hour delay." By that time we had to get up and drive to the airport.

At 9:00 A.M. we left for Barcelona. After a fast five-hour flight we boarded an unbelievably small plane to fly 100 miles over the Mediterranean to Majorca. The deep-blue sea, the fluffy clouds made me feel I was dreaming until the clouds parted and I glanced out my window and saw a mountain just four inches away from the wings. It was terrifying, but Majorca more than made up for our fright. It was brilliant and sunny, an island with beautiful old olive trees and masses of exotic flowers. We shared a car with an English couple from the Palma airport to the Hotel Formentor. The car was fueled by charcoal, which spewed a banner of black fluffy smoke behind us. The driver whacked the car the way one would whip a tired old nag, but the decrepit vehicle broke down every few miles. All five of us would climb out and beg water from isolated adobe huts where seemingly mute families crouched in open archways, their only diversion the winding road and infrequent passing cars. We made the day for them.

When we finally reached the Hotel Formentor, we were covered with soot. Art and I bathed, ate supper in a drowsy haze, then collapsed into twin beds swathed from ceiling to floor with pink mosquito netting.

The next morning Temple Fielding, the travel writer, dropped by and led us up a narrow mountain road to where he, his wife Nancy, and their six-year-old son Dodge lived. The Fieldings' house became our home base. It was a modern year-around haven for friends who stopped in day and night. I can still see a neatly piled mound of empty wine bottles at their back door—they were generous hosts—and their living room where one entire wall of glass brought the Mediterranean to our feet. Nancy ran her house from a sickbed which she'd moved into the den. She'd contracted a severe amoebic disease on their travels and Temple worried about her constantly. He was awaiting still another European specialist to fly to the island for diagnosis and hopefully a cure for her mysterious illness.

We spent ten days sunbathing on untouched natural beaches, watching flamenco dancers, eating suckling pig in cavelike bistros where Temple knew everyone from the family owner to the dishwashers. Twenty-seven years later I can still recapture my feeling of total contentment as I listened to my new and legal mate snoring softly every afternoon ("Siesta time! Come on, I'll teach you how to siesta") under his swaying pink canopy.

We tried daily to call my mother, but I think the overseas cable in Majorca ended five feet offshore. We reached her only when we returned to Paris.

ART: **It was a good honeymoon, though I don't happen to be an expert on them. I played a lot of Ping-Pong with two Americans in the liquor business, and made friends with the other guests. I did several columns on Majorca, which was still one of the hideaway places for American tourists. All the fears I had were subsiding, and I wasn't retching anymore. I'll have to admit it—I had a very nice time.**

The night we returned to Paris Marian and Irwin Shaw gave us a rousing welcome home party. Only Irwin could have foreseen our letdown in coming back to our dingy old rooms. "Thought you'd like to see how you used to live," he guffawed, knowing full well we hadn't yet found an apartment. The Shaws rounded up all our favorite pals, then added new faces who've since become close friends: Rose and Bill Styron, George Plimpton, who was in Paris that year helping to launch the *Paris Review*, and the Peter Matthiessens. The party went on till dawn.

I remember best one incident which had nothing to do with either Art or me, but rather with Irwin's magnetic appeal to women. As the party was getting into full swing, a glamourous—but uninvited—brunette made an impressive entrance on the arm of one of Irwin's pals, who should have known better. The woman was a well-known divorcée and gossip was that she had been making a serious play for Irwin. They'd been seen together at lunch and at sidewalk cafés from time to time that autumn; her name could never have been on Marian's invitation list.

But no one would have guessed the truth watching Marian's face. Her smile remained warm and welcoming as the woman approached. Only a few of us saw Marian deftly raise her right foot and with split-second timing trip the brunette at the precise moment she rushed past Marian to greet Irwin. Afterwards, Marian acted as shocked as anyone to see the elegantly dressed intruder sprawled on the floor, and was the first to help her to her feet, gathering up the scattered contents of her evening bag, smoothing her dress. Then Marian graciously ushered the woman to the door, and as far as anyone ever knew, out of Paris altogether.

Living at rue du Boccador was odd once we were married. Art's clothes remained next door in his old room. There was no kitchen. We couldn't visit between our two rooms without going into the hall or creeping along the outside balcony. I began to feel single again. We spent most of November looking for an apartment we could afford, in a central location since neither Art nor I knew how to drive. We were shocked to find that the French had built no new housing facilities for thirty years. Our only hope of finding a home of our own in the winter of 1952 would be through friends, hearsay, or luck.

One evening at an American Embassy reception I was delighted when a woman I'd just met, Lily Shepley, seemed genuinely concerned by my tale of woe. Lily was married to Phillip Shepley, a colonel at SHAPE; together they acted as a first-aid hot line for

Americans in trouble. Dark eyes twinkling, Lily whispered that there might soon be a vacancy in the building where she and Phil lived. A young couple named McKean was going to be transferred back to the States, but since they hadn't been told yet, Art and I would have to wait for a signal from Lily before trying to contact them. Lily did, however, tell us the address of the building: 83 quai d'Orsay. I automatically crossed my fingers since that section, just across the pont Alexandre, was one of the most beautiful in Paris, close to the Seine on the Left Bank. Even more important, it was only minutes away from both the *Herald Tribune* and my office on the Champs-Élysées.

A few nights later Art suggested that we go to a new restaurant on the avenue Bosquet. As we were finishing coffee he said, "So what would be wrong with just looking at the building? It must be right around the corner from here."

For a few moments we stood shivering on the street, admiring the outside of the five-story "hôtel particulier." It was handsome, well built, and in impeccable condition. Then we found a slight opening between heavy draperies on the street floor, and like hungry children outside a party, we took turns peeking into the apartment. We could see only two of its three rooms but they sufficed: exquisite wood-paneled walls, hand-laid parquet floors, a mammoth stone fireplace blazing with a magnificent fire. Taking one last look at the intimate dining alcove, the corner nook big enough for a desk and Art's typewriter, and two floor vents which meant central heating, I didn't dare hope. There would be a giant snag somewhere.

As it turned out there was more than one problem, but Art solved all of them patiently and cleverly, and one month later we were ready to move.

ART: **Compared to our two-room hideaway at 24 rue du Boccador the quai d'Orsay apartment was luxurious. Although it didn't have a view it was on the ground floor (people could look in instead of us looking out), it was located on the Seine, in walking distance of the**

Champs-Élysées and the *Herald Tribune.* The price was right about $150 a month. This was not much rent for an American, but was still very steep for the French. Also if memory serves me we paid in dollars which, in 1952, was the currency French landlords preferred, mainly because it went right into their mattresses with the gold, or so we were led to believe.

To this day people still swear the French hide their gold in their mattresses. If they do it explains why they're always so grouchy when they wake up in the morning.

Everyone had his apartment-renting story in those days. Our friends Jim and Maggie Nolan once rented an apartment in Paris for $500 a month. The landlord explained the rent was so high because he had very expensive paintings he was leaving behind including Modiglianis, Miros, and Matisses. About a month after they signed the lease they had a cocktail party and among the guests was the art critic from *Le Figaro.*

Jim proudly showed him the pictures. The critic went from one to another and all he said as he looked at each one was "Fake," "Fake," "Fake." There wasn't an original in the place.

Another friend was apartment-hunting one day and walked up five flights to a beautiful flat overlooking the Seine near the Trocadéro.

The lady who owned the apartment said, "It is so beautiful here. In the morning as the sun comes up you can see the barges going up and down the Seine. At lunch you can watch the fishermen and artists on the banks. As dusk comes you can see lovers walking along the quai. It's so beautiful—so beautiful—so beautiful—I've decided I don't want to rent it. Get out of here before I call the police."

One of the columns I got a tremendous reaction on

> **had to do with the film *Last Tango in Paris* with Marlon Brando and Maria Schneider. If you recall in the movie they meet in an empty apartment and commit all sorts of indecent sexual acts together. I explained the movie had nothing to do with sex, but was the story of two people competing for the same apartment. All Marlon was trying to do was humiliate Ms. Schneider so he could get the lease. When people saw the film in that light, they finally were able to understand it.**

We moved in the day before New Year's. Early in the morning we hired an old delivery truck and just dumped everything we owned into it, carton by carton. Then we rumbled across the river and feverishly unloaded the contents onto the living room floor before rushing off to work. That night we ate in a real kitchen for the first time in our married lives. After we were done, we unpacked, cleaned drawers and shelves with shiny white paper, and began to put away our things. It was exciting moving into our first home, and we worked right through the New Year. Art had been stuffing a leather hassock he'd bought in North Africa with crumpled *Herald Tribunes* when he fell asleep. I was puzzling over which closet would be Art's, which mine, when I heard a polite voice on the radio saying, "And a Happy New Year around the world!" It was coming from London. Because of the time difference we'd missed the birth of 1953 by an hour. Art heard the bells on the radio and tried hard to wake up. Without actually opening his eyes he kissed me, mumbled something about the "best damned New Year's Eve party I've ever been to," and flopped back into a deep sleep, his chin on his chest.

For the next four days we worked on the apartment. When we were finished it seemed like a miracle. The *Herald Tribune* gave Art a raise for being married, then the McKeans sold us—for a lump sum—several pieces of furniture which were more expensive to ship than to replace in the States. We acquired their double bed, their heavy oak dining table and chairs, their white sofa, and best of all the heavy silk draperies through which we'd first glimpsed the apartment. The rest of the absolute essentials we bought at the Flea Market on Saturday or the Prix-Unic, which was the French version of our dimestore.

It was on these shopping expeditions that I began to realize my inexperience as a housewife. I knew absolutely nothing about interior decoration. My only previous attempts had been as a child in a playhouse built by my Great-uncle Henry. He was my maternal grandmother's younger brother, and when his Ford auto dealership went bankrupt he appeared on our doorstep, seeking haven in the house where he'd been born fifty years earlier. My father made a deal to keep Uncle Henry busy and out of the way. "I'll buy the lumber and all the tiles and shingles you'll need if you'll pull down that smelly hen house and build something the kids can play in when it rains." Uncle Henry produced a splendid playhouse with three rooms we could stand up in, and with everything workable, even to the front porch doorbell. He then painted the interior a vile pea-green color which we reverently refreshed every spring for the next ten years. Twenty years later my sad conclusion was that Art, who had grown up in a series of foster homes, knew more about furnishing our apartment than I did.

He also seemed more at home than I in the kitchen. While we were still sitting around on packing cases I was struck with the thought: Here I am, the eldest of a family of eleven children, raised by a mother who spent most of her life in the kitchen, and I can't cook anything but fudge. I knew why. As our family grew—a new baby was born every fourteen to eighteen months—my mother had resorted to ingenious ways of stretching food to fill thirteen mouths three times a day. Noodle casseroles were prepared with only one can of tuna fish, meatloaves with more loaf than meat, peanut butter and deviled ham were thinned out for eleven lunch boxes. Somehow everything turned out delicious and filling, but had any of us been allowed to help Mom cook we would surely have asked questions and learned that we were poor. The result was that while we set the table and washed and dried dishes; we never actually prepared meals.

My cooking was not dreadful but not good either, and I had never tackled a range like the one in our new apartment. It had three settings. On ONE or TWO the heat was so low you could set a baby on the burner. On THREE it became hot enough to smelt ore. I tried to outwit the range, but usually lost. When I put eggs on to fry on TWO they stared at me like watery Orphan Annie eyes, uncooked. If I turned the switch to THREE the whites burned brown and leathery.

In those first months I was happy to discover that Art was a very good cook, and could make a lot of things including excellent coffee, without measuring.

ART: **The reader will discover as we go along that Ann is constantly putting herself down and giving me a helluva lot of credit for things I don't deserve. I naturally will accept all her observations though many of them have no basis of truth. I didn't know anything about decorating. Ann is good at it and will fight me for hours over a lamp or drapery color. I really couldn't care less but the fights seem to make her very happy, and I'd rather argue over a bedspread than something closer to the bone.**

I am not and was not more comfortable in the kitchen. I can cook if I have to, but it isn't worth a detour as they say in the *Guide Michelin*. Ann on the other hand is an excellent cook and a perfectionist. But this is her book and if she wants to make me the son of Escoffier, I can't do a damn thing about it.

As soon as we were halfway settled Art wanted to entertain. He loved people, loved to play host, but I trembled at the prospect of coping with French formalities and traditions. As recently as that week I'd heard the words "service plates" for the first time. At the moment our inventory contained one set of white ironstone china which would serve eight people if we washed between courses so plates could be used twice during a meal.

Still, at Art's insistence we decided to test my newly acquired skills one Saturday about a month after we moved in. To keep my nervousness at a minimum we limited guests to close friends, Dorothy and David Schoenbrun, Nancy and Teddy White, Fred Tupper with his girlfriend, a fellow from my office, and a visiting firewoman so thrilled to be in Paris she wouldn't have noticed if I'd served burnt toast. Art splurged and bought a large can of red caviar for hors d'oeuvres, then acted as bartender. Our apartment looked lovely. I'd filled it with flowers and dozens of candles. Everything went smoothly until the doorbell rang and Art ushered in Gregory Peck! Saying, "Hey, honey, I forgot to tell you that Greg was in town so I told him to drop by."

ART: **The tendency in those days was to pick up friends and bring them home unannounced. Strangely enough although many Americans had the run of Paris restaurants and night spots, few ever got into anyone's houses. I discovered tourists were all very curious how the French and Americans lived in Paris and were very flattered if you considered them good enough to ask them to come over. I knew I threw Ann by bringing home Gregory Peck, but I now know twenty-seven years later she would have been just as thrown if I had brought home Gene Moscowitz, a buddy of mine from USC.**

After years of being single we both had a lot to learn about being married. I never cured Art of bringing home unexpected celebrities, but I learned to cover my surprise. I also had to make personal adjustments. I was inexplicably tending toward helplessness now that I had a husband to take care of me.

One night while we were still unpacking I timidly asked Art, "Would you mind if I mixed myself a drink?"

He exploded angrily. "You don't have to ask my *permission*—this is your house and you can do anything you want, any time you want!"

I stood frozen by the portable bar, a wedding present delivered only hours earlier. Why the temper tantrum? I wondered. He rarely drinks; I was just testing his reaction to my having a Scotch and soda alone.

ART: **It's true I don't drink much. I like wine but having drunk up my life's share in the U.S. Marine Corps, I do not like hard liquor. Maybe I did blow up, but I suspect there is more to the story than she remembers. It had to be preceded by something. The problem I've had all my life is that I rarely blow up. It disturbs me more than the other person. I sulk a lot when I get mad and swallow anger like a box of Oreo cookies, which obviously is not healthy. What I may have gotten angry about is Ann's asking permission to do something which did not require my blessing. I must have felt she was testing me or something. Anyway since it sticks in her mind it must have been important to her or she wouldn't mention it now.**

Our constant traveling was another strain, particularly the first year. We were just settling in when Art had to leave for Belgium and I had to go to Spain for a Celanese fashion promotion. I dreaded being away from Art for almost three weeks and for the first time faced the problem of being a working wife—there would never be time enough to keep house.

ART: **Traveling was part of my job. You could get stale in Paris very easily and the readership in the *Herald Tri-***

bune were interested in all parts of Europe. My favorite towns for stories were London, Rome, Venice, and Vienna. (I went to Hamburg, Munich, and Berlin but never enjoyed them. It was still too early for me to see anything funny about Germany.)

The trip to Belgium was not for the column but to write English dialogue for a film the Belgians had made about shotguns. The Belgian commerce people offered me $200 to write this, which was a very nice sum of money.

We have to backtrack a little now. When I was going to USC one of my best friends and business manager on the *Wampus* magazine was a kid named David Wolper. When I told him I was going to Paris he said he was going into the television business. At nineteen years of age he figured out that in the early days of TV the stations would be desperate for film—any film—and he was going to get his hands on anything that people would sell. He started an outfit called Flamingo Films and eventually sold it for a bundle and then went on under various companies with his name on them to make such great shows as *The Making of the President* and *Roots*.

Okay, now back in Belgium. I finished the script and then was asked to do the commentary. The picture had already been done and I had to work with what they had. It ran about twenty-six minutes, although watching it it seemed like three hours. Most of the film took place in the shotgun factory in Liège and showed elderly men engraving the guns with hammer and chisel, rubbing the barrels to a shiny blue and fitting the triggers on to the stocks. The final two minutes depicted a hunter shooting a boar. It was a weird film, but $200 is $200 and I sold my soul by describing all these great

events with the thrill and emotion that Orson Welles puts into his TV commercials pushing Paul Masson wine.

After I finished the work the Belgians said, "What do we do with it now?"

"You mean you have no idea what to do with the picture after you've made an English version?"

"No, we were hoping you would tell us."

"Well," I said, "the obvious place for this masterpiece is on American television. It so happens I know the most important distributor of shotgun films in the United States. Perhaps I can persuade him to put it on his network. But it will cost you another hundred dollars."

They were thrilled and so I sent a cable to Wolper in Hollywood; the text read: HAVE TIED UP EXCLUSIVE AMERICAN TV RIGHTS TO BELGIAN SHOTGUN CLASSIC. WILL LET YOU HAVE THEM FOR $100. A day later I received a reply: WILL GIVE YOU FIFTY. It was typical of Wolper. I kicked myself for not asking for two hundred.

I'm happy to report that my Belgian shotgun film played during prime time in almost every city that had a TV station in those days—not once but dozens of times. If I made any contribution to the American scene while I lived in Europe it is that I gave the people in our country a sense of awareness of the tremendous skill it takes to make a Liège hunting gun. I've been proud of it to this day.

I thought Ann would be thrilled with the $350 I had made in Brussels, but like most wives she started grousing because I had been away so long.

With each of us away so often we became slapdash and disorganized. I bought a load of groceries one Monday morning and put them out on the balcony of our office where they sat for four days because

I'd immediately forgotten them. When I complained about our haphazard life Art interrupted, "Listen to how silly this sounds: I *have* to go to Belgium, you *have* to go to Spain, we've just returned from a wonderful week in St. Moritz, and you're in tears because your groceries have spoiled. We'll just *have* to learn to handle our hardships as they come!" It was true. Over the years I learned to treasure our freedom to pack up and go, leaving a sink of dirty dishes behind.

When it came to traveling, Art the married man didn't change a bit from Art the unmarried man. He had been lighting out for new adventures all his life, beginning at sixteen when he ran away from home, lied about his age, and joined the Marine Corps. He conned a drunken stranger into signing his father's name on the enlistment paper. He pulled a fast one on his father and sisters as well—sent them a telegram saying he'd joined the Army—in case they tried to trace him and drag him back.

In a certain sense, he also manipulated me. But even if I'd been aware of it, I wouldn't have objected. When Art traveled, it was for his work. "You'll profit indirectly," he always said as he packed his suitcase.

One day his boss Eric Hawkins took him aside and criticized him for leaving me alone so often. But Art just laughed when he told me, saying, "Isn't that just like Eric, the old bachelor worrying about somebody else's marriage."

During his absences, I would sleep and read a lot, get a new permanent, or later on when I was braver, even a new hair color. Then I'd buy a pretty nightie and pray that I wouldn't get the curse the day Art returned. Most of the time I was able to at least keep up a cheerful front, but sometimes I ached with loneliness and was sure I must be very poor company or Art wouldn't leave me so much.

Before we were married, we hadn't discussed Art's urge to roam and I usually had confined my comments to: "When will you be back?" and "Where is it on the map?"

Once when he told me "I'm going to Belgrade next week with the *Porgy and Bess* show," I asked, "Where is Belgrade?" "In Yugoslavia," Art answered. My next question was, "Where is Yugoslavia?" I felt like the joke going around Paris that year: An American movie mogul was flying around Europe looking for locations for a film. Disembarking in Rumania, he asked one of the ground crew, "Where are we?" "Bucharest," the local man answered. "I wish you'd decide on the name—first it was Belgrade, then Budapest, now it's Bucharest!" the mogul snorted.

After Belgium, Art left for two weeks in North Africa but in less than ten days he called from the airport in Paris. He had developed a strep throat in Casablanca and had hopped a plane home. As I fed him hot honeyed tea and tucked him into bed, he sank into sleep mumbling, "I really should have gone on to Tangiers, but what the hell, I didn't have any contacts there and I can always go next year," as if he were referring to a neighborhood theater.

At my request Art had bought us two small rugs in Marrakesh. I'd actually asked for a roomsize rug at least ten by twelve feet, but when I told him he had gotten the wrong size, he laughed and said, "Sew 'em together." Later he mentioned a handsome (but too expensive) Moroccan jacket he'd wanted to buy for me. "Tell me what it looked like," I suggested.

"Well, it was real short, about the length of our rugs."

ART: **It is a fact that newspaper marriages are not always the best ones because newspaper people by nature are far more interested in their stories than they are in their home lives. The good reporters tend to have short attention spans for domestic affairs and have a bag packed to leave at any moment. This was particularly true of American correspondents who lived abroad. It was a very glamourous life flitting from Algiers to Beirut to Moscow to Geneva. There were revolutions, summit conferences, and an occasional crisis such as Suez. The reporters had to be in the thick of it and wanted to be. Their wives, on the other hand, understood the job, but didn't like it. The sad part of it all was the women who were first attracted to the men because they did lead**

such exciting lives, were the same ones who learned to resent their work after they were married.

It wasn't just the fact of their being away that caused the trouble—they soon discovered the work was more important to most of these husbands than they were, and it was not much fun to play second fiddle to Tito or Khrushchev.

While I didn't cover wars or revolutions I endangered my life by attending film festivals in Cannes and Venice, went to Ascot and Buckingham Palace, covered fox hunts in Ireland, and sat through fierce tennis matches at Wimbledon. I searched for the Loch Ness monster in Scotland, played an extra in *Alexander the Great* in Spain (I was the one who bandaged Richard Burton's leg), took a bus from Algiers to the Sahara Desert, and went island hopping by boat through Greece. It was a tough life and Ann for some reason always thought I was having fun.

I tried to explain to her that the trick of the column was to keep moving and try to mix up the subject matter as much as possible. I told her if I stayed in Paris I would dry up.

What I didn't tell her is that if I took her with me we'd have to move in respectable circles, but when I went on my own the deeper mess I got into the better it was for the story.

Part of her knew this, but the other part of her didn't like it one bit, particularly when I looked so happy as I was packing to leave home. Every time she complained, my stock answer was, "You knew what I did for a living when you married me!" Come to think of it I still use that line and she still doesn't like it one bit.

Jealousy was the worst hazard I faced when Art left for exotic places. Once I went through every letter I could find in every drawer, briefcase, and carton in the study. It was terrifying, not because I found anything, but because—even though he'd called me that afternoon from Finland—I kept feeling he was going to walk in and catch me.

It was after that experience I decided I couldn't live with constant jealousy about Art's behavior away from home; it would drive me crazy. I would have to shut out imagined temptations like the starlets at the Cannes Film Festival who stripped off their bikinis at the sight of a newsman, and trust Art completely. I've worked at it ever since, even when Art's sole comment about an extraordinary venture consists of "It went okay," or when a catty friend—Art calls them "well-poisoners"—asks, "You mean he didn't offer to take you with him? How can you stand it?"

ART: **I never horsed around when I traveled—that I'll admit to. For one thing I was yellow and for another my picture was on every column and if I did horse around I knew it would get back to Ann in no time.**

I recall once telling her, "If I'm ever stuck somewhere and can't call you because the lines are down or there are no phones—I'll take out a girl and in twenty minutes someone will telephone you to tell you what I did, and you'll know I'm all right."

Though I gradually adjusted to Art's travels, one time I did blow up. Art had called jubilantly from Monte Carlo right after Grace Kelly's wedding. He had been one of the few newsmen who had actually witnessed the ceremony. At the last minute, Father Tucker had sneaked him into the church despite Prince Rainier's edict banning the mob of reporters who had gathered from all over the world. Only a few correspondents and a handful of favored magazine editors had been allowed in the church. It was sweet revenge for Art who, the day before, had been left stranded on a slippery hill he was climbing with Ben Bradlee of *Newsweek* and Crosby Noyes of the

Washington *Star*. The three had sworn to stick together, but as the path grew steeper and rain began falling, Ben and Crosby had spotted a French journalist driving a tiny Volkswagen. They'd jumped in the car, slammed the door, and hollered out the window, "Only room enough for two. Sorry, Artie!" and sped off. Now Art was wallowing in triumph. Suddenly his voice changed and he said, "You're not laughing, honey, you sound strange. Is anything wrong?"

"Oh, no," I answered acidly, "not in the sense of international headlines." Then I screeched, "TODAY IS MY BIRTHDAY, that's all, and you didn't even remember. I don't care if Grace Kelly got married and divorced all at the same time!" And I slammed down the receiver.

Usually I took Art's travels with good grace, but sometimes I wondered if he would ever feel really married. Once right after our second anniversary he set out for what was then the Belgian Congo, a long and difficult trip at that time, and one which frightened me. He would be away for almost a month, doing a daring but funny feature for *Collier's* magazine called "Coward in the Congo," a photo reportage of Art on safari, big game hunting with bearers, jungle beaters, and handsome white hunters. Their itinerary was two pages long and involved multiple airline changes at unpronouncable airports before they would arrive in Stanleyville, their takeoff point for the wild trek. For days I waited nervously for news. At last, a letter arrived bearing African stamps. It was addressed to *Miss Ann McGarry*.

I tried not to cry, but the truth was that from the moment we stood in the doorway of Westminster I was aware that while I had ended Art's bachelorhood, he would never become a conventional husband leaving for work every morning and coming home promptly every night at six. He would always want to feel free to travel. A part of him would never be tied to home, wife, and children. How large a part I wasn't sure and in the early years I was sometimes convinced we had made the mistake of our lives by getting married. But just as I was ready to weep because I couldn't run home to mother, Art would surprise me with a little note of funny verse reaffirming his love. He always wrote what he was never able to say: that he was happy.

Still I've never taken him or our marriage for granted, and often under his more humorous messages is a hard kernel of truth. On our first anniversary he gave me a painting he'd commissioned from a *Herald Tribune* artist: two cherubs flying through a field of hearts and flowers trailing a banner with the words "Can this marriage be saved?" On our fifth wedding anniversary he gave me a $500 check and a card saying "Each year of marriage has been worth at least $100 to me. I'm running away from home; don't try to find me. I'm re-enlisting in the Marines under a false name. Please explain to the kids. I was never meant to be married anyway. We've had a lot of laughs and I think we should be grateful. I hope we can still be friends." A few years later my anniversary flowers came with the note "I don't care if we are married—we still seem to be living in sin." And on our twenty-second anniversary: "There are 24 roses here, 22 for when it was legal and 2 for when it was illegal."

And on our silver anniversary, tucked into a pile of presents was Art's passionate tribute: "It only seems like twenty-four."

Five

Almost from the day we returned from our honeymoon, I began counting the days until I got pregnant. I thought constantly about having a baby—what a relief to know I was free to do so; it was okay, we were MARRIED—and every month I prayed for pregnancy. The moment my period was a couple of days late, I would dash over to the rue de Berri laboratory for a rabbit test. Without telling Art, who had begun saying "when we have a baby" as often as I thought it, I would patiently wait the necessary forty-eight hours before going back to the lab and nonchalantly requesting my test results.

When month after month went by and nothing happened, I was puzzled. Being the first of eleven children, and the aunt of three of my younger sisters' babies, I had never doubted that I could have as many of my own as I wanted.

After the first false alarms I confided in my old friend Ginette Seidman, who arranged for me to go to her gynecologist, a French doctor well known for his work in infertility. He also loved gossip, so that as I lay in ignorance and terror on his stirrup table I was forced to answer questions about whatever parties Art was currently covering. When he'd finished both his excruciating treatment and the final details of a dinner he'd attended the night before, he said, "Now hop down from the table, and in three months you'll be back to tell me you're pregnant. I fixed everything."

Despite his promise I counted off three more months of disappointing menstrual regularity, and began listening to whatever far-fetched advice I was offered. One Catholic friend assured me I would become pregnant if I slept with a picture of Saint Theresa under my pillow. I decided I couldn't explain that to Art and instead made a Novena to Saint Theresa, going for nine consecutive days to early morning Mass in honor of the Little Flower, pink or blue, it didn't matter. Then a French friend divulged a family secret handed down for generations. "It's very simple." she said. "You must have sexual intercourse while you are standing on your head."

Later I resorted to medical books and began keeping detailed monthly charts with thermometer readings which would determine my fertile days. The only hitch was Art's constant traveling, usually for only one or two days at a time, but invariably the same days my chart indicated that I was on target.

Late one morning I called Art from my office and said apologetically, "I just realized you're leaving tonight for three days—so this is our ONLY day."

"Now? Before lunch?" Art queried in disbelief.

"Now," I whispered into the phone as I reached for my coat to dash out the door.

Art and I arrived at our apartment within seconds of each other. We ran into the bedroom as if pursued by demons, ripped off our clothes, and then remembering that the cleaning woman might have come in that day, scurried from room to room making sure we were alone. Back in the bedroom, still huffing and puffing, we took one look at each other and fell onto the bed, helpless with laughter. After a while we realized we couldn't stop giggling long enough to make love, we gave up, dressed, made peanut butter sandwiches, and went back to work.

* * *

ART: **This is something a woman would remember and a man would forget. It isn't that I have any objection to making love in the afternoon, it's just that I don't recall the phone call. I believe I did want children at that time, but I don't think I was desperate about it. I figured it would happen sooner or later. I also must admit I thought it was strictly a woman's job to have babies. I was willing to cooperate up to a point, but my sex education was limited and I assumed when a woman was ready to have a baby she'd have one. I'm not being facetious now, I'm being honest. We never used any birth control devices before the marriage. Yet for some reason I was never worried that Ann would get pregnant.**

After we got married I assumed she would and I can't ever remember asking myself how come it never happened. Babies were very important to Ann. Having come from a family of eleven I imagine it was more important than she even knew. On the other hand I had never known my mother and therefore I suspect I didn't want to know too much about the whole process. (Years later when I was on the couch I discovered that I had some serious hangups about actually producing a child. The idea scared me more than I would admit.) This is not to say I wouldn't have welcomed a baby, but I wanted it delivered in a nice pretty box, and I certainly didn't want to cause anyone pain having one.

If this sounds dumb, so be it.

When I told Ruth Ascarelli my closest friend and confidante what we had gone through, she sent me to her thyroid specialist. He tested me, strapped me into an oversized chair with wires worming out its back, locked a metal collar around my neck, pushed a button, and said, "Ninety minutes and you won't feel a thing." Then he walked out of the room, closed the door behind him, and left me to scream until he sent in his secretary, who sat staring at me as if I were a retarded child. Twenty treatments later, five every week for a month, I was still not pregnant but blessed with an overactive thyroid for which I have taken medication ever since.

When my treatments seemed fruitless, Art agreed to go with me for a series of tests at the American Hospital. Dr. Lester Lipsitch, the head of the hospital and our good friend, summed up the inconclusive results. "Your best bet is to keep trying. Although you haven't asked me about adopting a baby, I think I should warn you that in France there are two prerequisites: a couple must be married for at least ten years and be over forty years old. You don't qualify on either of those counts."

ART: **What Ann didn't say was Dr. Lipsitch told us I was the problem. I had a very low sperm count. He claimed if I lost weight it might go up. But he had no magic pills. In spite of the fact the good doctor said all this in front of Ann she has on occasion still blamed herself because she could not give birth to her own baby. There are a lot of devils and goblins in these Irish Catholic women particularly when they don't fulfill the role of natural mother.**

Art went off to Geneva that night and I went home, vowing to be patient and keep praying. But when Art returned and we were having a quiet candlelit dinner, he cleared his throat and said in a low, gentle voice, "I talked to the Cooneys today about adopting a baby from Ireland. Dick said he would contact the hospital in Dublin where they got their little girl. Ireland has tightened up on adoptions but he said he and Mary Ellen would do everything to help us."

I had often seen little Joyce, the Cooneys' pretty pink-haired infant at Sunday Mass. And I was fully aware of how that baby had helped Mary Ellen pull out of a depression when she learned she could have no more children. But their case was different—they already had two young sons.

Listening to Art's suggestion, the unspoken word "abnormal" echoed in my head. I was a woman with a part missing . . . an "irregular," to be marked down and put on sale, like a faulty item in a store. I was incapable of following Art's careful explanation of what we would have to do to apply for a baby from Dublin. Instead, to his surprise I began sobbing. I wept for myself, and for Art who would never have a son with his exact genetic makeup. Fortunately he refused to take my remorse seriously and continued making plans, for while there was no way I could have known it on October 12, 1953, perhaps at the very moment Art and I had been passionately celebrating our first wedding anniversary, a baby boy was born in Ireland who would eventually become our oldest child.

ART: **Adoption to me sounded like a dandy idea. The baby would come in my nice packaged box. Besides I felt, and still do, that it isn't by whom the child is born, but by whom it's raised that counts. I never for a moment doubted that if we adopted a baby it wouldn't be mine. To this day I can say honestly I've never had any fantasies about what my blood children would be like as opposed to my adopted ones.**

My three children are MINE. They belong to me—at the beginning we were tied by a legal adoption paper. Now it's an emotional bond on their part as well as mine. I love them deeply and they've given me the same share of happiness and heartache that I'm certain my blood-born children would have.

I recall once making a speech to a group of adoptive parents and I said, "You know adopted children are *really* yours the day you forget they're adopted and think: "these kids are a real pain in the ass." Everyone

in the room applauded because they knew it was true.

Like pregnancy, the adoption took nine months. We began by meeting with Paris authorities who could help us: Father Daniel Sheehan who spoke for the Catholic Church and John McCloskey who represented the Catholic Welfare Association which would have to pass on our application. Then came the legal work: Notarized applications, birth and marriage certificates, letters of reference for the Dublin orphanage and the Irish government. Finally late one night we received a call from Dublin. A happy woman's voice said, "We have a little boy for you; his name is Joseph."

When I could speak, I asked, "What does he look like, Sister?"

"Ah, he's a lovely, lovely lad," she said and economically hung up.

Two months of unexplained delays followed. We later learned that the head of the Irish Passport Office had gone on an extended vacation immediately following the nun's call. We thought we were being rejected; the truth was that all the paperwork piled up on his desk, unprocessed, until he returned.

When we finally received a telegram from Dublin confirming all was in order, we immediately flew to Ireland, arriving in the coldest, most depressing week of the year: the first in February.

ART: **A small point of disagreement, but that's what marriages are made of. We didn't get word that all was okay. We got no word, and I suspected that we were being given the brush-off. So I told Ann the only thing to do was to go over and press the issue. I decided that once we were on the scene we could pry that baby away from the Irish one way or another.**

When we did get to the orphanage the nuns were not happy to see us and asked why we didn't wait until we had gotten the okay. I said we couldn't wait. He was

> ***our* baby and we didn't want him to spend one more day in an orphanage than he had to. As far as I was concerned that boy was *ours*, and they had no right to keep him. The nuns, rather than becoming surly, seemed delighted that we cared that much. Besides, they hated red tape as much as we did. They were on our side during the entire battle to whisk our "first born" out of Ireland.**

When we reached Dublin we checked into the Russell Hotel, tossed our luggage into our room, which we noted was as cold as a meat storage plant, and hailed a taxi. "Take us to Saint Patrick's Hospital as fast as you can!" Art shouted.

The driver raced through traffic and stopped in front of an old rundown stone building with the words ST. PATRICK'S chiseled above its doors. We weren't aware that it was the wrong St. Patrick's until we walked up to ring the doorbell. The place was ominously silent. Puzzled, we pushed our way through some half-dead bushes to the back of the building, hoping to find someone who could tell us where to go. In our haste to get to the hospital we'd left the street address in Art's briefcase, which was, of course, back in the hotel room.

As we neared an open window we saw a room crammed with young boys. As soon as they spotted Art they swarmed over to grasp his hands and touch his face, shouting, "Come on, come play, tell us your name, tell us a story." We were later told that these were boys who had grown too old for adoption—everyone wanted *babies*—and that they would be brought up together in that one building until they were old enough to be sent off to work. The only grown men they had ever seen were priests; men in musty black cassocks who smiled or frowned but were always too busy to play games. And you don't touch priests. Art had to promise that he would come back some day and tell them a story before we could get away to find the babies' hospital.

* * *

ART: **As I looked at those little fellows I couldn't help seeing myself at the Hebrew Orphan Asylum. It was not my type of scene.**

After a frustrating hour during which we found a St. Patrick's *something* on almost every street in Dublin—dry cleaners, cinema, grocery store, barbers, let alone chapels and churches—we stopped at the right place. A white-robed sister opened the door and said, "Surely you must be Mr. and Mrs. Buchwald; we've been waiting for you." She was Sister Frances Elizabeth, head of the hospital: young, pretty, with a soft voice that I will remember as long as I live.

She led us through a nursery filled with newborn infants in white iron cribs. I was dazzled by the beauty of one wide-eyed infant whose name card said "Anthony." Sister Frances allowed me to linger only a few moments before she said, "Little Anthony is beautiful, but because of his heart he will not live much longer." Then she swirled her white skirts toward the exit and led us down a long cold hall which opened into an even icier sitting room, bereft of both furniture and carpeting. Our baby sat at the end of a cavernous room, quiet and composed as a Buddha, waiting for us. His hair was a brilliant orange-red, his eyes bright gray-green, and although we knew that at sixteen months he could barely crawl, his face was as flushed as if he'd been running for hours. He was dressed in several layers of clothing; two or three sweaters under a jacket, heavy wool pants which looked cut-down from those of an older boy, and tightly laced leather shoes.

He neither smiled nor cried, but sat motionless on the floor beside the empty fireplace and silently studied Art and me. We dropped to the floor, hugged him, hugged each other, hugged the sister, all of us speechless until Art said, "Look at the red car we brought for you to play with." Joseph's eyes solemnly followed the toy as Art pushed it back and forth. Then for the first time a tiny smile curved the baby's sweet mouth. It would be fun to teach him more about happiness.

* * *

Our own joy was nearly erased when we returned to the hotel. A message was waiting from the Irish government forbidding us to take Joseph out of the country. On the day before our arrival in Ireland, the Minister of External Affairs had surprised the country with a decree: "We will no longer allow babies to be our principal export. No more adoptions except to citizens of Ireland." We were in danger of losing our baby just when we'd found him. We were aware the adoption situations had gotten out of hand. One successful American career woman, when asked what her friend could bring her from Europe, had said, "A baby from Ireland." And although neither woman was married at the time, the New York executive did indeed get her baby. But we did not feel such casual excess applied to our own case.

ART: **One of the difficulties at this time was that movie actress Jane Russell had just adopted an English child and there was a big scandal about it in the British press. The story of American movie actresses taking children off to the United States suddenly attracted the Europeans' attention to the fact that they were losing their children to American families. Since the U.S. was not that well loved in Europe the "adoption scandal" was an easy target for the media as well as the politicians. The problem was that Europe was still getting on its feet and the Europeans weren't making any great effort to adopt their own. Also adoption has never been accepted as well in Europe and Great Britain as it had been in the United States. The Europeans put a lot more currency in knowing the bloodlines of the children.**

As time went on and Europe became more prosperous the available sources of children for adoption dried up. I was involved with the International Social Service which took on the task of helping American families find children from abroad. In the early sixties it was

> **almost impossible to get any government to allow their orphaned nationals to be sent to the U.S. I'm not criticizing them for getting tough about it. The wealth of any country is still in its children.**

The moment we got the bad news, Art began calling our Irish congregation: Sybil Connolly, the fashion designer; Father Cormac Daly, pastor of Adam and Eve's church, whose parish included St. Patrick's orphanage; Liam Boyd, manager of TWA for Ireland; plus dozens of reporters. They all hinted that we would be wise to steel ourselves for a turndown. It looked hopeless as I sat over dinner our third night in Ireland, salting a tasteless meal with my tears.

Art said, "Stop crying and I'll tell you my plan. We'll fly directly to Monte Carlo from here, and ask Rainier to let us adopt a baby from his orphanage."

"And leave our baby here in this cold country?" I sobbed. "What will happen to him while we're away?"

Art, who had initiated the idea of adopting an Irish baby—"You're Irish and Catholic; you'll be able to raise him exactly as you would any baby we would have"—and who had engineered every maneuver we had made for nine months, agreed we should not give up. "But next time," he added, "maybe we should try Monaco."

We'd spent a week the previous summer in Monte Carlo where we'd met Prince Rainier, still a carefree, handsome bachelor surrounded by bikini-clad beauties who were continuously being kicked out of his life by his pastor and confessor, Father Francis Tucker. The fun-loving reverend was an American priest who had lived in Monaco for years, and knew every syllable of gossip in the Principality. One night at dinner he boasted that he had just ejected a French movie starlet who had come dangerously close to dragging the prince up the aisle. "She'll never step foot on this soil again," he said with a wink.

During our stay Prince Rainier himself had taken us through the Monaco Orphanage, which he personally supervised and financed.

He visited it daily and knew the names of every child in the place.

But memories of that sunny week did little to console us as we waited in the cold rains of Dublin for permission to remove little Joseph from the hospital and for a passport to take him out of the country. Neither came.

Father Daly suggested we plead our case personally with the Archbishop of Dublin. He set up an appointment, warning Art that he would be expected to greet the Archbishop by kissing his ring. Art hesitated only a moment before saying, "For the baby I'll do it, but I'll be damned if I'll kneel!"

Still, after a half hour with the Archbishop, we left more downhearted than ever. "You must understand our problem," the prelate had said. "How can we be certain the baby will be raised in his own religion when only one of you is Catholic? Then, too, there is the difficulty about where you live, two Americans residing in *Paris* . . ." and we both knew the Archbishop was visualizing can-can girls and smoky bistros.

The next morning Art was waiting at the TWA offices when they opened to see if Liam Boyd could perhaps do something. Liam said, "By coincidence I went to Trinity College with the Minister of External Affairs. He's pretty tough but I can try appealing to him on a strictly personal level—he owes me a favor or two." Liam then gave a handwritten note to a messenger boy with instructions to hand it personally to the Minister and to bring back a reply.

Art waited in Liam's office, trying to make small talk for nearly an hour, until the cyclist returned with the Minister's response, also written by hand. It consisted of six words: "All right, but just this time." We will never know what college prank Liam dredged up from the jolly past to force him to concede.

ART: **The trick in Europe when it comes to any kind of red tape is to push the right button. Liam was our button. I think the Minister did it as an old-school-tie favor. In**

> **any case, wherever you are Liam we shall never be able to thank you enough.**

We knew we would have to change the baby's name because Art's father, Joseph Buchwald, was very much alive and the Jewish religion forbids giving a newborn infant the name of a living relative. I told Art that I wished Catholics obeyed the same ruling. Within my own family there were so many Pats, Marys, Joans, Susans, Jackies, even Anns—named for sisters, great aunts, grandmothers, and my mother—that we had begun using all three names, first, maiden, and married, to tell them all apart.

At first we decided to call our baby Adam, a name we associated with Marian and Irwin Shaw's exuberant three-year-old son. But then we realized that for sixteen months our baby had responded to Joseph so we decided that his new name should sound as similar as possible to the only one he had ever heard. Joel seemed perfect and Joel he became.

With the baby's legal papers and passport clutched in our hands we hurried from the Department of External Affairs to the hospital and bundled our baby into a taxi almost before the nuns could wipe away their tears. At the last moment, Sister Frances beckoned to me. "I have a special favor to ask," she whispered as she led me down a hall and into a vast linen closet where hospital bedding supplies were stacked to the ceiling. "No one ever writes to us, and it's so sad not to know how the babies look as they grow up. We have only one photograph . . ." she reached under a pile of muslin sheets and extracted a black-and-white photo of a pretty three- or four-year-old girl standing beside a rosebush in front of a white ranch house, "somewhere in the state of New Jersey."

I promised that we would be different. We would write faithfully and send pictures at every new stage of the baby's development. How cruel, I thought, not to do so when that was all the sisters asked in return for their months of love and tireless care.

Back in Paris I did write three letters to Sister Frances. One reported Joel's first steps when he teetered from my arms into Art's as if the floor were a tightrope. Another described his first "boy haircut" after one too many strangers stopped us on the street saying, "*She* has the most unusual and beautiful shade of red hair!" But as I reached for a photo to enclose with the third letter, I suddenly stopped. I knew exactly why no one had ever kept in touch with the sisters. From the moment we'd held Joel in our arms, he was ours. I didn't want to remember the orphanage. I wanted to forget the sixteen months when hands other than mine had nursed him. I tore up the letter, put the photos back in my desk drawer, and never wrote again to the sisters.

On our way to the airport we asked the taxi driver to keep his meter running while we scurried up the steps of Adam and Eve's church. Father Cormac Daly had told us he wanted to give Joel a special blessing. The priest took Joel in his arms, whispered a brief prayer in front of an altar dedicated to St. Anthony, the miracle worker, and handed him back with best wishes for our trip home.

All the while we'd been in Dublin Art had been distressed by the redness of Joel's face and hands. He had said, "The first thing we'll do when we get home is take him to a good doctor; there must be a cure for whatever rash is making him so blotchy."

"I think that rash is what you call frostbite," I said. "If we ever get him warmed up, his face and hands will turn out to be a normal shade of pink." By the time we reached Orly Airport, Joel's tear-stained face was no longer red—in fact, it was gray with fear. He had been terrified by the noise in the small nonpressurized plane and had cried hysterically through the two-hour flight.

ART: **"Damn it," I said to myself as I looked at that beautiful blond (red head?) little boy, "I have a son. I really have a son. He sure doesn't look like me, but he's the spitting image of Ann." I saw in him a first baseman, maybe a quarterback—though if he wanted to become a doctor I wouldn't stand in his way. I wasn't much on fishing or hiking, but when he started to walk he could come to**

the office with me and use my typewriter and I would be able to say to everyone, "I want you to meet my son."

I think I was also rather frightened by the whole idea. When you start a family you've got responsibilities. I wasn't afraid of the financial ones, but I was of the emotional commitments. Up until then Ann and I were just playing house. But once a baby came in the picture—one we practically kidnapped from Ireland, marriage started to get serious. I wondered if I was up to it. But the joy of having a son of my own made this concern fade from my mind as our plane headed toward Paris.

My chief concern when we got home was about Joel's meals. Sister Frances had warned me against changing his diet too quickly. "He has been fed only three things in his life: milk, porridge, and bananas. It would be so nice if we could have given the babies orange juice, but citrus fruit is so dear in Ireland. However, if you could manage to give him an orange once in a while . . . I'm sure he will love it."

Two decades later I asked Joel, who was watching me fix dinner, if he liked bananas, adding "I can't recall ever seeing you eat one."

"Nope, I hate 'em, always have—why?"

As parents we were like converts to a religion which everyone else had long taken for granted. We moved to a larger apartment next to the hotel Plaza Athenée and hired then routinely fired a series of stern old professional nursemaids called "nannies," convinced none was good enough for our child. We did at last find one we liked, a gentle young French girl named Michèle who arrived at 9:00 every morning and left at the end of the afternoon.

Art took on more work at the *Herald Tribune*. At one point he was writing or contributing to three different columns. He also sought out assignments from American magazines—*Look*, *Life*, *Collier's*—which paid him in dollars that could be converted on the French black market into more value in francs. By 1955 twenty-two American papers were running his column regularly.

We were now a household of five—two parents, one baby, a part-time nurse, and a wonderful full-time Oriental housekeeper, Tsien. Salaries were: Tsien, $40 a week, the nursemaid, $18. Our rent for a three-room apartment plus kitchen and servants' quarters was $150 a month.

Tsien lived in one of the small rooms set aside for servants on the top floor of every French apartment building. One morning he sent word that he was sick and unable to work so Art and I prepared a tray of food and took it up to him. We were shocked by the conditions the French seemed to think acceptable for their help. Tsien's room was like a cell with no heat and no running water. The only light was a dim bulb hanging from a cord in the ceiling and there was no carpeting or linoleum on the bare floor. For the next week I measured and shopped in a bustle of American outrage. By the following Monday, Tsien had a bright linoleum flooring, a new mattress, warm blankets, a lamp, a radio, and a line of plumbing bootlegged from the communal bathroom at the end of the hall to provide him with privacy as he sponge bathed. There was no bathtub for anyone on that floor.

With Joel comfortably adjusting to his new home, my days took on a routine very different from when I had been working full time. Michèle, the nursemaid, arrived every day to clean Joel's room and to do his washing and ironing. Since no French apartment had a washer or dryer, we ended up stringing everything on racks in the kitchen. The result was that the clothes absorbed a mélange of odors from whatever had been cooked during drying time. I finally became so nauseated by fishy-smelling nighties and blouses reeking of french fries that I began drying my personal laundry behind the window curtains. One morning a stranger from across the open court of our building rang our doorbell and asked me the price of "the pink robe in the middle window." She thought that I'd hit upon a clever way to sell things from home.

While Michèle did our chores, I set out with Joel in his carriage to do the daily shopping. There were no charge accounts in France; we paid for everything in cash and took our purchases with us. No store delivered anything less weighty or expensive than a piano. And every shop specialized in its own line of food: the crémerie for milk, butter, eggs, and cheese; the bûcherie for meat, another store for fish; the pâtisserie for cookies, tarts, cakes; the boulangerie for bread and croissants; and still another store for fresh fruits and vegetables. The only shop I never went into had a horse's head mounted over its front door. It sold horsemeat. I used to lower my eyes when I went by to avoid looking inside.

ART: **When I first came to Paris I used to eat horsemeat steak. I liked it. Then I found out *cheval* meant horse and I crossed it off as one of my favorite dishes.**

Wheeling Joel from shop to shop, I'd heap my bundles into his carriage until only his face showed through the pile of pharmacy purchases, dry cleaning, baby shoes, hardware supplies, and food.

My strategy was to make the vegetables and fruit store my last stop, because whatever I bought would be handed to me in loosely furled newspapers. Several times a week Joel would arrive home in a bed of spinach or with green beans sticking out of his sleeves.

Tsien rearranged our kitchen and converted one dark, roomy cupboard under the kitchen sink into a miniature "rec" room for Joel, who sat in it for hours, bashing pans and banging spoons, while Tsien cleaned, mopped, cooked, and chopped. He scorned the nursemaid, in fact any woman with whom he had to work. He loved Joel and was possessive to a degree we couldn't understand until he confided to Art that when he was forced to flee North Korea he had left behind an illegitimate infant son.

* * *

ART: Tsien played an important role in our early marriage and a difficult one later on. He was every man's dream of the perfect manservant. He cleaned the house, took care of our clothes, and cooked the best Chinese food of anyone we knew. Paris was short on good Chinese restaurants though there were many Vietnamese restaurants on the rue Monsieur le Prince on the Left Bank. Our friends, for the most part Americans who lived in Paris, were all Chinese-food freaks (you can even OD on French food if you have to eat it every night), and so when we entertained Tsien went all out. Afterwards our friends would come to the house and tell me in Tsien's hearing that we should put him in the restaurant business.

Tsien did not understand English, but he understood what they said and in the back of his mind that is exactly what he wanted to do.

One day Tsien came to me and said that he would like to someday go into the Chinese restaurant business.

I told him that someday if he ever found a proper location I would help him finance one.

The next day Tsien returned and said he found one.

Suddenly I lost my manservant and found myself raising $50,000 for a Chinese restaurant on the rue François 1er, off the avenue George V.

I went back to all the damn people who had said we ought to put Tsien in the restaurant business and sold shares (one share cost $2000, a half share cost $1000). My shareholders included John Huston, Anatole Litvak, Faye Emerson, Irwin Shaw, Al Steele (then president of Pepsi-Cola), and Darryl Zanuck. We put up the money in dollars but cashed them on the black market for an extra twenty percent premium. This was one of many mistakes I made because the French authorities kept bugging me as to where we got the money for the restaurant. Also as time went on we had all sorts of legal problems with estates of backers who had died. Their executors wanted their money in dollars.

My good friend and lawyer Charlie Torem had set the whole thing up so I was the only one who could go to jail.

Tsien, that gentle soul who loved my son and had been a loyal and humble servant, became a tiger once he was planning his own restaurant, which he named "Chinatown."

My second big mistake was letting a girlfriend of my buddy Jim Nolan do the interior decorating. She was a good decorator but Tsien insisted, and I believe now he was right, she didn't know one thing about a Chinese restaurant. He anguished, screamed and begged me to get rid of her because she was using up all our funds on color schemes, when the money should go into the kitchen. I was too close to Jim to fire the lady, and for years Tsien never hesitated to remind me of what a muckup she made of his place.

I was also haunted by Harry Kurnitz, a screenwriter and famed raconteur who rented my apartment one summer when Tsien still worked for us. Harry told so many amusing stories that he got credit for many he didn't tell. After the restaurant finally opened, I ran into a friend on the avenue des Champs-Élysées who said, "Hey, I hear you put Harry Kurnitz's chef into the restaurant business."

I found a lot out about human nature as the president of a Chinese restaurant syndicate. People will give away money, gamble it as if there was no tomorrow and spend it insanely on women. But when they have an investment they demand dividends, and raise bloody hell when every bowl of rice isn't accounted for.

Darryl Zanuck, who used to bet $2000 on one hand of chemin de fer at Deauville or Monte Carlo, had his office manager call me up every month if his $40 dividend check didn't arrive. Tola Litvak was the same. He thought Tsien was stealing. Since the restaurant only sat thirty-five people, if he was he was welcome to it.

Once Al Steele's lawyer came to see me after Steele died and wanted to see all the books relating to the $2000 investment. I showed him what we had and as a good lawyer he said he needed more information. I lost my cool and said, "Listen, you son of a bitch. You're going to use this visit to see me to write off your entire trip to Europe as a business expense, so get the hell out of here and sue me."

I never heard from him again.

There were many funny stories involved with "Chinatown." One had to do with Darryl Zanuck when he was courting Bella Darvi. He took her to "his" restaurant but there were no tables and he didn't have a reservation. Tsien said he would have to wait. This was too much for Darryl's pride.

He stalked out in a rage and called me the next morning, saying as an owner he deserved to be seated immediately. I told him there was nothing I could do about it, and besides if he had the true spirit of an "Owner" he should have been happy the place was full.

"I'll never go back again," he vowed.

Years later I ran into Darryl in Paris and asked him if he ever went to "our" restaurant.

Darryl, cigar in the side of his mouth, blew up.

"That Goddamn Chinese restaurant. I'm in the process of separating from my wife Virginia, and we worked out our entire financial settlement. Then her lawyers heard about my investment in the restaurant and hit me for $10,000 more." It took everything in me to keep a straight face. All I could say was "Wow, I didn't know our shares had appreciated that fast."

When Mike Todd was opening *Around the World in 80 Days* in Paris, he told me, "I want to give the after-theater party in your restaurant."

"For God's sake, Mike, the restaurant only holds thirty-five people. We can't handle a post-première party."

"Don't worry about a thing," he said. "I'll keep it small. I want champagne, booze, and everything on the menu. Money is no object. We go first class."

With trepidation I told Tsien to pull out all stops. His little kitchen couldn't handle it but we decided we could use the money.

Sure enough Mike invited about 100 people all in black tie and bejeweled up to their hair buns. Elizabeth Taylor, Mike's wife, was with him. The food was late, Mike was screaming, and I finally put on a white jacket and played the role of a waiter pouring champagne and even running around the corner for pizzas.

At 2:30 A.M. the nightmare was over. Mike told Tsien it was one of the best parties he had ever given. Tsien stood there with a bill for $1,200 in francs. Mike made no effort to grab it. I gave the bill to Mike and he said, "Come over to the Hôtel Meurice at ten tomorrow morning and I'll pay you."

Elizabeth, as she kissed me good night, whispered in my ear, "We're leaving for Rome at seven."

I went home, set my alarm for six A.M., got dressed, grabbed a cab to the Meurice, and called up to Mike's suite. "Hi, Mike," I said, "I couldn't let you leave without saying goodbye."

"Come on up, you bastard," he said.

I walked into the suite waving the "Chinatown" bill.

Mike, who had plenty of money, still got his kicks out of figuring ways of not paying his debts, said, "Who the hell told you I was leaving early?"

Elizabeth said, "I did."

Mike looked at her and said, "If you weren't so beautiful and I didn't love you I'd leave you to starve in Paris."

Long after I went back to the U.S. the woes of "Chinatown" plagued me. We finally sold it to Tsien, who paid our investment back and gave us six percent on our money.

It is the first and last time I ever got involved in the restaurant business. By the way I lost about $8,000 of my own money so people wouldn't sue me and open a can of beans to the French fiscal authorities, who to the very end were curious as to what all those famous Americans were doing as partners in a small nonprofit restaurant on the rue François 1er.

While Tsien was still with us and the household running smoothly, we settled down to enjoy our new baby. Art's reaction was to spoil him relentlessly. Every day Art brought Joel a new toy. I murmured warnings about spoiled children but was completely defeated by our American friends, who sent us lavish gifts from the United States. On Art's first trip back after adopting Joel, Hannah Troy and Mollie Parnis gave Art a baby shower. We still have a photo of him dressed in a frilly bonnet, cigar clamped between his teeth, the only man in a roomful of women, buried under an avalanche of expensive infant clothes and toys. Al Steele, who as president of Pepsi-Cola had spent that spring in Paris, ordered one of his executives to hand-carry from New York the best present of all: the first baby butler we'd seen, a plastic table with a canvas bucket-seat and ball-bearing wheels which, with the slightest push from Joel, shot him up and down the hallway like a Le Mans racing driver.

Every afternoon, following Joel's daily airing, I would present him like a crown jewel to the women I'd invited for tea—visitors from the States, wives of Art's colleagues, women I'd worked with. No one escaped. When people came for cocktails Joel crawled around their feet. When we had small dinners, he sat in Art's lap.

One night we took out Marlene Dietrich, who was in Paris to shop for her costumes. At Art's suggestion, I resolved to talk about something other than our amazing new baby, but to our surprise all Marlene wanted to discuss was children and housekeeping. Oozing glamour, she shared her experiences as a mother, her secret recipes, and some of the best tips on running a household I'd ever heard. "You should see the way I shined up Maria's apartment last month in New York," she said. "Cleaned it from top to bottom, even waxed the floors, left it beautiful!"

As her car pulled up at our apartment building at the end of the evening, Art said, "Tell the driver to wait for five minutes and come see our baby!" It was past midnight as we tiptoed into the apartment, roused Joel, and brought him out for Marlene's approval. She took one look and exclaimed, "He has no idea how lucky he is, see that long line between his upper lip and his nose? He will be very handsome . . . no matter what good features a man may have, if he has a short upper lip he will never be more than 'cute.' "

ART: **Marlene was a legend and also a Jewish mother. I guess you can be both. I was happy to be in her company. She was full of sexy stories about Hemingway, General Omar Bradley, Erich Remarque and everyone else I had ever heard of.**

She was one of the biggest stars in Europe and women particularly would stare and envy her, even though that sexy throaty voice was aimed at the men in the audience.

One night I went to her opening in London at some fancy café. She brought the house down. I walked backstage and found myself in a mob of admirers from Laurence Olivier and David Niven to the Duke and Duchess of Quelle que Chose. Then after all the "Dahling's and "You were mahrvelous's, the room started emptying out, and before I knew it I was the only one left with her.

There was no party, no beau, no nothing. The performance was over and no one thought to ask this sensational woman if she was free after her show.

We went back to her suite at the Dorchester, just the two of us, broke open a bottle of champagne, and talked until four in the morning.

Art's special time with Joel was on Sunday mornings while I went to Mass and shopped for the day's fresh bread and milk. He would lug Joel, stroller, and an armful of toys down five flights to avenue Montaigne and together they would set out on a round of visits to the Hôtel George V, the Prince de Galles, the Ritz, Plaza, Continental, wherever our American friends were staying. Most often they ended at Fouquet's sidewalk café on the Champs-Élysées where Joel sat eating ice cream while Art and his pals gossiped and tried local cures for hangovers.

One Sunday morning Art took Joel directly to the Lancaster Hotel to visit Elizabeth Taylor and her husband Mike Todd who were in Paris on one of their many visits. Art's call from the lobby must surely have wakened them; we have a photo of Elizabeth lying in bed, her head propped up on one elbow, smiling at Joel, whose eyes are riveted not on the most beautiful woman in the world but on a glistening trinket she had left on her nightstand. His face reflected such jaded disinterest that everyone who saw the snapshot burst out laughing.

Americans had begun bringing their children to Paris with them. Irving and Sylvia Wallace brought seven-year-old Amy; Lucille and

Desi Arnaz brought little Lucy and Desi; the Russell Crouses brought Tim when he was eleven years old. On those Sundays Art would take the gang to the Jardin des Tuileries, where they rode ponies in the park, or to the Paris Zoo, where the animals were allowed to roam freely behind elegant wrought-iron enclosures.

ART: **Paris was made for children. The parks had puppet shows, pony rides, swings and large sand piles. Disneyland was manmade, to turn a profit. The parks of Paris, and there were dozens, had been designed to make French life worth living. Sailing a boat in the Tuileries can be as much fun as going down a roller coaster. Joel still remembers our Sundays in Paris, but better still—so do I.**

Whenever Art was away, he would send Joel daily postcards, even when he was so small he thought they were something to chew on. Then one spring day Art came back from a trip and said, "You know as well as I that we're spoiling that child so badly he won't have a friend in the world when he grows up. There's nothing more rotten than a spoiled brat. I think we need another baby; I don't want to raise and ruin an only child. Let's start looking for a little girl."

It was June 1956. Joel was barely thirty-two months old. We again asked Dr. Lipsitch for help but he reiterated that we were still ineligible to adopt a French baby. A few days after his gentle but definitive turndown, Richard Condon, then a press agent for United Artists, later a very successful novelist, called from Spain and invited us to spend a week in Madrid, where he was publicizing *The Pride and the Passion*. He assured Art of material enough for a series of articles on the making of the film, and on its stars Cary Grant, Frank Sinatra, and Sophia Loren. I vividly remember meeting Sophia, who was just learning English. She was sitting under an ancient olive tree, her lap full of first- and second-grade storybooks, reading aloud to a circle of men who seemed riveted by the tale of Henny Penny.

The film, based on a book called *The Gun*, was being shot in an

800-year-old walled city called Àvila, twenty-five miles outside of Madrid, where the townspeople had allowed Stanley Kramer, the director, to remove all telephone poles, electric wiring, and other signs of the twentieth century in exchange for his using most of Àvila's inhabitants as extras in his film.

A young Spanish publicity woman named Conchita Castelli was assigned to drive Art to the set each day. As they bumped along the dusty roads Art asked her about adopting a baby in Spain. She said we had a chance. She knew the director of a big orphanage in Madrid and added that Spain was swarming with babies born out of wedlock as so many couples were too poor to marry. Art promised we would name a baby girl after Conchita if she helped us pull it off.

ART: **The trip to Madrid had actually started as a junket. A junket for those who don't know it is when a movie company or hotel picks up the tab for a newspaperman. In the 50s junkets were more acceptable than they are today. I took them mainly because the *Herald Tribune* in Paris was not about to pay my expenses to go to Madrid, and the Trib bosses had no objections if someone else did. In this instance United Artists never did get its money's worth since *The Pride and the Passion* was a bomb, even with Miss Loren and Grant and Sinatra.**

While we were in Spain we became good friends with Grant and his wife of that time, Betsy. As a kid I had idolized Grant and imagined myself as the suave good-looking romantic character he usually portrayed. He was a very fascinating talker and also outspoken when he felt like it. One night in a restaurant in Madrid a man came up to him and asked for his autograph.

"Put it to my wife, Cary," the American tourist said.

Grant was livid. "Why do you want this signature?"

"Because she won't believe me if I say I saw you if I don't have your John Hancock."

Grant stared him straight in the eye. "What kind of relationship do you have with your wife that she wouldn't believe you if you said you saw me in a Spanish restaurant?"

The tourist disappeared.

Cary and Betsy—particularly Betsy—were very interested in our attempts to get a baby. Cary didn't want children and I think Betsy was hoping our success could influence him. A side note—Betsy left Madrid to go home about that time and took the *Andrea Doria* on its fateful voyage. I heard about it in Madrid, called UP, and found out Betsy was safe. I kept calling Cary at the Palace Hotel but he was out shooting. I finally got him around seven in the evening. His first reaction was "Is she all right?" His second was "Did they say if she had lost her jewels?"

On our last morning in Madrid, word came that the director of the orphanage would grant us an interview. Art, Conchita, and I arrived within an hour, and Conchita translated our request: "We would like to see only newborn babies, please." A parade of nurses began bringing in baby after baby, some only a day or two old. Art and I squirmed as we looked at the minuscule bundles—they all looked alike. I wondered why I felt so bewildered. I had seen four of my younger sisters and brothers when they were only hours old. In fact, I'd seen my sister Jackie almost immediately after she'd been born because I'd been hiding in my mother's closet to eavesdrop; I wanted to find out what was happening to my mother.

But nothing from my past seemed of any help in making a choice. Art finally begged Conchita to have the director halt the procession until we pulled ourselves together. The director was delighted. He had a live American newspaper reporter all to himself. That, in fact, had been the real reason for granting us the interview—he wanted public recognition for his hospital. He opened a large leather scrapbook and began showing us photographs of his new equipment. At the end of the album he turned a page and said to Conchita, "Tell them that this series shows what miracles we can now perform. Look at this infant we found abandoned and near death on the outskirts of the city. We baptized her at once, naming her Matilda for the saint whose feast day had just passed. Here she is at one month, still frail, here at six months, getting well, and here at one year—a picture of perfect health, saved by our new equipment and methods!"

A beautiful, round-eyed girl's face shined up at us from the page. Without pause I exclaimed, "Where is that baby NOW?" To our astonishment, the director closed the album and looked away. Then he brusquely gestured to a nurse waiting in the corridor to resume bringing in more babies. Art whispered to Conchita, "Tell him you have to call your office, but go and find out about Matilda."

An hour passed. We had run out of comments and Art barely glanced at the continuing stream of infants. As each one passed we repeated, "We'll wait to find out about the baby Matilda, if you don't mind." The director by then was as nervous as we were, and indicated by pointing to his head and to his spectacles that he would personally check on her whereabouts. As he went out one door, Conchita came in with a smile of wicked triumph on her face.

"The director knows very well that Matilda is still here," she said, glancing at his departing back. She is his pet and Sister Superior says he doesn't ever want to let the baby go. But don't worry, I said a few things I won't translate and they are bathing and dressing Matilda now. She will be here in a minute."

The three of us sat lined up alongside the absent director's desk, waiting in silence. Then we heard a stir and turned to see two nuns holding up a beautiful little girl so that she looked as if she could stand alone. She was dressed in a white hand-embroidered organdy dress over two or three lace-trimmed petticoats, bright red shoes, and a pair of tiny gold earrings. As we stepped out onto the terrace the nuns suddenly released her hands but instead of pleasing them by trying to stand, little Matilda angrily thumped her fat bottom down on the flagstones as if to say, "Stop showing me off; I'll walk when I want to, not a minute before."

We scooped her up and carried her outside where we spent an hour playing with her under the trees. Conchita told us that her appearance had been delayed because the hospital owned only one fancy outfit, which they used when presenting any little girl to prospective parents. Sometimes I wish we had had the good sense to offer the hospital a yearly donation in exchange for that glorious outfit, but we didn't and they're probably still using it.

It was the last day we could safely linger in Spain without jeopardizing Art's job. We had found the baby girl we'd hoped for, but at the same time discovering that of all the infants in the orphanage we had chosen the only one its director was dead-set against relinquishing. Before we left he painted a black picture of the battle we would have to wage for her papers and passport.

That night we had dinner with Richard and Evelyn "Red" Condon in their Madrid apartment. Both Condons promised to follow up on our passport application for the baby, now named Conchita Matilda, and to visit her every day until her papers were approved. One official had sworn it should not take longer than ten days.

But our main hope lay in Conchita. As she drove us to the airport Art said, "You're not only the godmother of the baby, you're now our field commander."

Back in Paris we bombarded Madrid with affidavits and notarized character references. Weeks passed. We placed long-distance calls and sent cables to everyone short of Franco, but none of the officials responded. Conchita's progress reports to us became more depressing each week—she was getting nothing but alibis and runarounds. We cursed the Spanish for their four-hour siestas and complicated, disorganized bureaucracy which made the French system seem as simple as boiling eggs.

One morning, as Art was getting dressed for work, he shouted, "Goddamnit, I'm going to fly to Madrid tomorrow and get that baby myself!"

Four days later Art called from Madrid airport. "I've got our baby right here in my arms, we're leaving in five minutes. Meet me at Orly Airport at three o'clock." Just before hanging up, he added, "You'll never guess how I got her!"

* * *

ART: **The big stumbling block was the Spanish passport and exit visa which all nationals needed to leave the country. The Spanish passport people were having none of it as far as Matilda was concerned. I went down with Conchita and we both ran into a red-taped stone wall.**

Conchita left with me and said, "I have an idea. Let's go back to the orphanage." We returned and she said to the nun, "Lend us the baby for a few hours." They trusted us, dressed up Connie in the one dress the orphanage kept for all babies, put the one pair of earrings they kept for their children on her, and off we went back to the passport office. I carried Matilda in my arms and Conchita walked up to the desk, pointed at her and said to the officer behind the desk, "This is who we want the passport for."

Everyone in the office melted. The officials who wouldn't give us the right time gathered around Connie and started cooing to her and speaking endearments in Spanish. In a half hour we had our passport and in a few more hours I decided to get the hell out of the country before the Spaniards changed their minds.

Once again I had to face a tearful scene at the orphanage with the nuns crying and Connie not too thrilled about leaving the only home she ever had.

We made one stop at a children's store and bought some clothes and a few toys. The dress and the earrings, of course, had to stay at the home for future candidates for adoption.

Ruth Ascarelli drove me to the airport. As we roared into the parking lot we saw Art strutting back and forth, holding Conchita Matilda in his arms. She was wearing a new white organdy dress, the nearest Art could come to the one we'd first seen her in, and lace-trimmed rubber panties. She seemed completely untouched by our excitement, and was happily hugging Art's neck.

It was the twenty-eighth of July. In October Joel would be three years old and we had told him we were going to bring him back an early birthday present. When we got home, he was waiting for us in the doorway of his bedroom. We placed Conchita in his outstretched arms. She had been so well fed by the adoring nuns that she weighed only ounces less than Joel, but he determinedly hung on and with knees buckling managed to carry her to his room where I'd squeezed a second crib next to the washbasin.

ART: **Not long after we brought Conchita home, I told Eddie Albert, the actor, about the orphanage. He was looking to adopt a little girl and since he and his wife Margo spoke Spanish, he was willing to try Madrid. They looked at the babies and then saw a wistful, beautiful four-year-old playing in the garden.**

"What about her?" Eddie wanted to know.

"She's very old to be adopted," Señor Mellado warned.

"She'll get older if she stays here," Eddie said.

Eddie and Margo went up to her. The four-year-old's name was Maria and she was very belligerent and defensive. Apparently she had gone through the adoption routine many times with no success.

"How would you like to come home with us?" Margo asked.

Maria shrugged. "It's all right with me. But you should know one thing. I shit in my bed."

Maria is now in her early twenties, one of the most delightful and beautiful young ladies I know. She found her home and Eddie and Margo found their happiness.

One week after baby Conchita settled in, the telephone rang as I was about to go out. It was Dr. Lipsitch. Without any warning he said in a totally matter-of-fact voice, "I can't—and won't—say any more except that a baby is due to be born here sometime in September. After all the hounding, you and Art are entitled to first choice if you still want another child. Do you?"

Still clutching my gloves and purse, I managed to say, "Give me five minutes to call Art?" Then I hung up and dialed Art at his office. "Are you sitting down? Lester Lipsitch just phoned—he offered us a baby who will be born sometime next month. He'll need a girl's name and a boy's name for the birth certificates. Should I give them to him?" I held my breath and waited for him to drop the phone, but after the briefest pause, all Art said was, "Of course; call Lester and tell him YES."

ART: **For someone who was afraid of responsibility I was certainly gathering a family very fast. I have always been a fatalist and I believe it was written somewhere that we were to have Joel, Connie, and Jennifer as our children. The idea of one child may have frightened me, but having two or three I discovered, didn't throw me half as much. I even remember thinking to myself, "I'll bet the way things are going we may even wind up with one of our own."**

Jennifer Marie Buchwald (we'd submitted the name Jeffrey in case the baby turned out to be a boy) was born at 7:00 P.M. on September 16, two weeks later than expected. She weighed only 4.4 pounds, so she was immediately whisked into an incubator where the doctors insisted she stay until she weighed five pounds. Two weeks later, rolled up in a giant ball of cotton with just her tiny heart-shaped face visible, she was pronounced healthy enough to be taken home, but with the proviso that we engage a registered nurse to take exclusive care of the new baby for thirty days.

While Jennifer was still in the hospital, I worked frantically with rental agents until I found an apartment large enough to house our expanded family. It was one half of an elegant old town house, directly across from the beautiful Parc Monceau. An elderly French couple owned the building but lived ten months a year in their country château several hours away from Paris. For all practical purposes we had the place to ourselves except for December and June, when our landlords appeared and sniffed around. The rental agent said, as we signed the lease, "Since the owners are childless, they were very hesitant about your two babies, but I finally convinced them to let you have the apartment." I realized that fortunately we had overlooked telling the agent about Jennifer's birth.

We hastily moved into 52 rue de Monceau and proudly presented Joel and little Conchita to the concierge. Two weeks later, Dr. Reginald Kiernan, head of pediatrics at the American Hospital, sauntered up the staircase to our first-floor apartment and handed us Jennifer, curled up in the bottom of a small market basket. Weeks went by before the concierge caught me by my sleeve and said angrily, "You and Monsieur moved in with two enfants, but now I count three!"

As soon as Jennifer arrived, we converted the dining room into a temporary nursery and closed it off from the rest of the apartment. The nurse would not let us enter without gauze face masks, and for a month she was the only one allowed to bathe and feed the baby while Art and I stood watching wistfully from the doorway.

Within nineteen months, between February of one year and September of the next, we had three children, each perfectly spaced eighteen months apart. And for two years after that we had three babies in diapers. One morning without advance warning the owners of the only diaper service in Paris presented us with an award for using the most diapers in the history of their company. They arrived at our door dressed in their best suits, determined to make a ceremony of the presentation. Art and I, still in our bathrobes, stood frozen while the president of the company delivered a formal speech and handed us a parchment scroll with a blue ribbon attached. When they left we howled with laughter until we saw the number of diapers we were paying for every week: 280!

As soon as the children were old enough to understand, we told them where they had come from, how we had chosen them, and why. They became so bored with the story that one night when Art tried to entertain them at bedtime with the story of their adoptions, Joel burst out angrily, "Not that one, Daddy, tell us a REAL story!"

ART: **Ann and I, however, never tired of remembering how we got the children. In no instance was it simple. Jennifer was made a ward of the state until the papers were approved. This took six months. One week Ann had advertised for a cleaning woman and was interviewing several, one right after the other, when a nice-looking French lady came in the living room.**

"Let me see your references," Ann said.

The lady looked puzzled.

Ann did not notice her discomfort. "You will have to do washing, ironing and we can only use you three times a week."

The woman at last was able to speak. "There is some mistake. I am the social worker for the French Adoption Agency and I've come to do a home study to see if your apartment is big enough for another child."

The lady didn't mind being mistaken for a cleaning woman and we must have passed the test.

A retired judge was appointed Jenny's ward until she was ours. We invited him to the apartment and poured drinks into him for two hours while he looked us over. Oddly enough it wasn't as tough as I thought it would be. You may not be able to get married in France very easily if you're a foreigner, but the adoption process, particularly with the American Hospital's blessing, was almost a breeze.

Jennifer was the only child who came to us as a newborn infant. Therefore as a father with no experience with babies I was frightened of her at the beginning. She seemed so small and fragile I was afraid to pick her up. I

was also fearful something would happen to her. I would sneak in and peek at her when no one was around. Sometimes I would talk to her. "Hi, stranger. What stupid person would give you up?"

People who didn't know any better thought Ann and I had cleverly planned to have a child from Ireland, Spain, and France. What they weren't aware of, and it wasn't worth explaining it to them, was that the children could have come from anywhere. Once they were in our house their origins had no interest for us. As a matter of fact we wanted to make them Americans as soon as possible just on the off-chance that some woman would come to the door and say, "I want my baby back."

No one did, but the fear, which I kept to myself, was always with me when they were small.

Visitors rarely guessed the three children's countries-of-birth. Without fail, someone would look from one face to another and say, pointing to Jennifer's curly black hair and dancing brown eyes, "Well, you can certainly tell which one was born in Spain!"

"No," I'd reply, "Jennifer was born in France."

Connie, on the other hand, looked like a native Californian with her violet-blue eyes and sun-streaked hair. When she was three years old, Art finally gave in to my pleas to legally shorten her name. "After all, I insisted, "how can we ask a little girl to grow up explaining a name like Conchita Buchwald?"

Even Joel confused a few people, who insisted he looked English though I never understood why. He not only looked a little like me, and a lot like my red-haired Irish father, but his ears stuck out so jauntily he could have passed for a leprechaun if we'd dressed him in green.

Soon after Jennifer was born, we began receiving regular visits from a government agent who handed us 25,000 francs a month—roughly $50—merely because we had three children. The French government, eager to increase the country's population after World War II, subsidized all families with children, and went so far as to encourage women to have babies out of wedlock. The government paid all such maternity costs, all hospital and medical bills, and whenever a mother agreed to care for her baby in one of the government's special homes, seven months of free food and lodging for both mother and child.

We tried for three months to convince the agent that we didn't need the $50, adding that surely another family would appreciate receiving our share. But the agent, one side of his jacket stuffed with cash, the other with messy little notebooks, stood his ground. Our refusal would cause him grave trouble, he complained. His books wouldn't balance, and he would lose his job. In the end, we gave in, and gracefully pocketed the cash, enticing the poor man to at least stay for a glass of wine. He thought we were crazy.

What if we had not found our children or worse yet, having found them not been allowed to take them home where we knew they belonged? That we did bring them safely home seems just as miraculous as their birth itself.

I'd been ready for motherhood all my life. Before I could ride a two-wheel bike I could bathe, feed, diaper, and tend a baby. While I was so young I was still swallowing my grandmother's stork stories, I loved every new baby my mother brought home from the hospital; I'd moved over for ten of them.

Art's childhood memories tugged at him in a different way. He wanted a family to match what he'd merely imagined over the years when he and his sisters were separated.

Once we were parents we found living in Paris had a special advantage. We could spoil and enjoy the children any way we would. We had no relatives nearby to criticize or take over. Most rewarding was their love for each other. Joel hovered over Connie like a secret serviceman while she played in the sandbox, Connie wheeled Jenny's carriage the moment she herself was steady on her feet, and Jenny offered to punch anyone who bothered Connie in kindergarten.

ART: **It didn't last. When they got old enough they clobbered each other all the time.**

* * *

When we got off-track, or the children did, Art and I had terrible fights. But he always sided with the children, patiently explaining to me exactly why they had misbehaved. Despite anger and disappointment, at times, neither of us could spank them or find any fault which wouldn't vanish in a matter of hours.

They formed and filled our lives even more than we did theirs.

Six

"We are not expatriates," we exclaimed whenever anyone used the word, "we are Americans living in Paris." There was an enormous difference: expatriates were people who abandoned the country of their birth, an inconceivable thought to us in those years.

We loved our country. It had allowed us to question ourselves—our careers and futures—and to come to France in search of answers. We knew very little about anyone's past history, but while we compared notes on what date and by what means we'd arrived in Paris, we never asked each other why we had come.

Perhaps it was because none of us knew precisely what we had hoped to find in Paris, apart from distance. We had dared ourselves to go—and gone while our courage was high—confident that we could return to the States whenever we chose, find other jobs, and settle down.

At first we felt impelled to do anything we pleased and knowingly squandered time, money, and emotions for days and sometimes weeks. Some Americans arrived in Paris to last only a few months, a summer or a spring, before hurrying home, but those of us who stuck it out became deadly seriously about our work. Two common goals, survival and success, bonded us together. We formed friendships as durable as those made by people who live side by side for decades.

The majority of our American friends worked in communications, for newspapers, magazines, radio networks, publishing houses, or public relations. Many, like Dorothy and David Schoenbrun, had arrived before us. The Schoenbruns had come in 1947 when the city was still shivering and hungry after World War II, and they introduced us not only to such celebrities as Jean Monnet and Jack and Mary Benny but to many couples who subsequently became our closest buddies.

ART: **The postwar II American generation in Paris has not been glamourized in the manner of the Americans who lived there during the thirties. Perhaps we had no Ernest Hemingway or Gertrude Stein, but we did have James Baldwin, Irwin Shaw, Peter Matthiessen, George Plimpton, James Jones, Janet Flanner, Mary McCarthy, Allen Ginsberg, Man Ray who spanned both generations, Alexander Calder, and even Julia Child who taught cooking in Paris.**

We all had our own little cliques but I'm certain we had as good a time as Americans who lived in Paris in the twenties and thirties. Perhaps the legend of the postwar II generation hasn't had enough time to blossom, but I'm defensive about it, and I always felt sorry for the people who came to Paris in those years and tried to relive Ernest Hemingway's life.

The city attracted every type of American after the war. I knew black marketeers who used to sit in the bar of the George V and sell carloads of sugar to Yugoslavia in exchange for coal from Germany, and diverted U.S. Army PX supplies from Frankfurt to Spain. There were

used-car salesman, and Bernie Cornfeld selling mutual funds to GIs. One fellow—an American press agent named Guido Orlando—used to hang out in the plush hotel lobbies drumming up business. He would dream up stunts for prospective clients on the spot.

The one I liked the best took place in Deauville. I ran into Guido nervously pacing up and down the lobby of the Hôtel Royal. "I think I may have King Farouk for a client," he said.

Farouk, who may have changed the history of the world because his excesses gave Nasser an excuse to overthrow him, spent his evenings in the French gambling casinos losing millions of francs. His losses and his life style were the stuff that gossip sheets all over the world lived on.

Guido explained that he had been talking with Farouk's aide de camp and had persuaded the aide Farouk needed a new image. Orlando proposed that he call a press conference and announce that when Farouk gambled he was trying to win money for the widows and orphans of Egypt. At that very moment the aide was up in Farouk's suite presenting the proposal to the king. I decided to wait around with Guido for the answer. It came about an hour later. The aide de camp returned to the lobby red-faced and said to Guido, "His Royal Highness told me to tell you that what he wins he keeps!"

Besides con men and Americans on the make, there were poets holed up on the Left Bank, writers hoping to finish a great novel, painters who planned to set the world on fire, and CIA agents who were infiltrating every organization they possibly could. It isn't generally known, but the CIA financed the *Paris Review* and countless European travel guides. They also gave free plane tickets to American students so that they could observe Communist youth rallies, and managed to get their people jobs as foreign correspondents as well as put legitimate newspapermen on their payrolls.

I recall in 1967 walking down Fifth Avenue and running into a reporter I knew in Paris. We started talking about the good old days in France. "You know," I said, "all the years you worked in Paris I thought you were a CIA agent."

"Isn't that funny," he replied. "I always thought you were."

F. Scott Fitzgerald could have had a ball with some of the Americans we knew in those years. Dr. Reginald Kiernan, our pediatrician, had a fight with the Board of the American Hospital and they refused to renew his contract. This made it impossible for him to practice medicine in France. Rather than leave, he became a male model, posing for French magazine advertisements. Then Simone Signoret decided he should become a movie star. He made a couple of French movies, got terrible reviews, and couldn't get any more work in films. Still determined to stay in Paris, Reg spent years in the snooty Traveler's Club on the avenue des Champs-Élysées winning enough money at backgammon to keep him in good clothes and good humor.

Then there was Eddie Constantine, a young American singer who became a protégé of Edith Piaf (read boyfriend). He did not have much of a voice, but he had a scarred face and wound up playing a tough-guy American in French detective films. The French loved him and he became a millionaire. He was the Humphrey Bogart of France.

Many Americans came to Paris because they were

driven out of the United States during the McCarthy years and could not find work there. Larry Adler, the harmonica player, was one. He and dancer Paul Draper were accused of being Communists. They both sued the lady who accused them—won the suit, but never the less were blacklisted and couldn't get booked in a theater in the U.S.

There was Jules Dassin, the talented director (*Never on Sunday*) who also was blacklisted and had to leave, along with Ben Barzman, a fine screenwriter, and Michael Wilson. Fortunately they found work in Europe.

We had divorcées who came to Paris with their children to get away from their husbands, and wives in Paris who got divorced and stayed on because Paris had become more home than the United States.

There was even a time when the IRS had a ruling that if you lived abroad for 18 months you didn't have to pay United States income taxes. Suddenly movie stars started to take up residence in Paris, London, and Rome. They saved on taxes but most of the movies they made were not hits, so they hurt their careers.

One of the great attractions of Paris in those days was that with hardly any money you could travel a few hours' distance by air and be in another culture. You could go to Switzerland, or England, or Italy, or Greece. In the U.S. if you flew from New York for an hour you'd wind up in Detroit.

I haven't covered all the types of people we knew, but it was a mixed bag. We had the bond of being Americans, plus the confidence that we were truly the best and the brightest. After all we were American—and that spoke for itself. Little did any of us dream, that like Farouk, the dollar would someday not be king.

* * *

It was David Schoenbrun who was responsible for our own few moments of international fame, by putting us on the television show *Person to Person*. Edward R. Murrow, who hosted the program, wanted to interview an American family living abroad and David suggested that we were certainly lively and interesting.

CBS had decided that Charles Collingwood would narrate the *Person to Person* program since he was then head of their television division in Europe. That made us feel even more at ease; we had known Charles and Louise Collingwood for years. "It'll be a breeze," Charles said. "We'll show a typical American couple living in Paris; the highlight will be three little children eating a typical French meal." We all agreed that the first course should be a cheese soufflé.

On the morning of the actual filming, our recently weather-stripped windows were thrown open and long cables were snaked through them from a mobile van on the street. Art and I huddled together with woolen bathrobes over our clothes. We had instructed Kay Walsh, our nursemaid, to keep the children in their warm bedrooms until noon, and to feed them nothing after breakfast. It was imperative that they EAT when the time came. Danielle, our cook, began making a cheese soufflé at 11:00 A.M. It would be perfectly puffed by noon. Noon came and went. Danielle gestured from the kitchen that the soufflé hadn't long to live; so I asked her to make a second one. At two o'clock another soufflé died in its fluted dish. The technicians were still working and Charles asked me once again to change my dress— "Sorry, wrong color, and no way of hiding the wires to your hidden microphone."

Finally three hours and two soufflés later we began. Kay released the children from their rooms and they raced to the table like starving animals. Joel picked up his portion of the soufflé and held it high over his head like a sword swallower. Connie refused to lift her eyes from her plate, her delicate left hand shoveling food to her mouth without a second's pause. Jennifer pounded her spoon and fork on her highchair tray, enraged because once again she was being served last.

ART: **The only thing I remember, besides the kids eating all the food served to them, was showing off a chess set. It had a great deal of sentimental value because I bought it from the wife of a political prisoner when I was in Belgrade. The woman, a friend of a newspaperman stationed there, needed money. Her husband had carved the chess set while in jail. I don't know where he got the knife, but while not attractive, it did have political significance. There were no bishops, kings, or queens. The bishops had been replaced by army officers, the king by a general, and the queen by what could only be described as a female member of the politburo.**

***Person to Person* was then one of the biggest TV shows in the U.S., and all my pals as well as our families saw the "tough" life we lived in Paris. I thought it was great. When I left the U.S. many of them predicted I would never make it. What better way to prove they had been wrong than to make them sit through a TV tour of our fancy digs in the City of Light. A foster child never forgets.**

The longer we stayed in Paris the more we were obliged to entertain visiting firemen. "Call the Buchwalds first thing," they'd been told. "Here's David Schoenbrun's home telephone number," "If you get in any trouble call Charlie Torem," "The Bernheims know Paris inside out—Alain was born there," "Just ask our PR man, he'll get you front-row seats," "We have a whole bureau at your disposal, use it!"

We rallied and helped each other. "Ed Murrow's arriving tomorrow," "Danny and Sylvia Kaye will be here for a week," "Betty Bacall is in town without Bogie."

I was always a nervous wreck when we were due to go out with famous people for the first time, and I envied Art his easy-going manner with celebrities whose names alone tensed up my stomach muscles. Art already knew most of them. He'd either met them on a trip, had lunched with them or interviewed them for his column. But his self-confidence didn't rub off on me. I reverted to the small town girl—Warren, Pennsylvania's nearest real celebrity came from twenty miles away: Lucille Ball from Jamestown, New York.

I loved meeting people who matched names I'd heard and read about, but wished I could be invisible, free to look and listen without responding. Imagining an evening ahead, I'd feel nothing was good enough. I'd rearrange furniture in the living room when people were going to come to our apartment for cocktails before a night on the town. Or I'd break into tears of frustration or despondency, neither of which Art understood. "What are you worrying about, everything looks swell!" he'd say as I plumped pillows, dusted the piano or rummaged in my closet hoping to find a miracle. "Just wear a suit, we're only going to a little bistro," was his solution to almost every evening's dilemma.

It was unthinkable to be anything but a fan with the likes of James Thurber, for instance. One evening he and his wife Helen came back with us for a nightcap and he sat until 3 o'clock in the morning telling stories about his early days at *The New Yorker*, occasionally missing an ashtray by an inch and stubbing out a cigarette on the arm of a chair. It didn't matter; he could do no wrong, I was sickened by the fact that he was blind.

Gradually I began to realize that people came to see Paris, not to check up on me. And another thing: the bigger the star, the more famous and secure the celebrity, the nicer and simpler person it turned out to be. One afternoon as I was changing Jennifer's diapers, the front door burst open and Art hollered in, "Guess who's with me. Thornton Wilder! He wants to see the baby." Thornton Wilder was in Paris that month for the first French production of *Skin of Our Teeth*. He had lots of time to kill every afternoon. I slapped a blanket around the baby, pulled off my apron and plunked Jenny into the playwright's waiting arms.

One night, however, I learned that even a pro can get the jitters when facing something new, and the experience helped me lick my fear of not measuring up.

Alfred Lunt cooked a ten-course gourmet dinner for us in our own kitchen. The Lunts, Alfred and his wife Lynn Fontanne, then acknowledged as the most illustrious husband-wife acting team in American theater, had come to Paris for the summer so that Alfred could enroll in the Cordon Bleu cooking school. It was a lifetime ambition, he told Art, and furthermore he promised Art that he would prepare a feast for us and a select group of friends the day after he earned his diploma from the famous academy. I forgot all about it until one Wednesday evening when Art said, "Alfred Lunt has finished his course and is coming over Saturday to prepare the dinner he promised us."

Panic set in. I looked at our kitchen through Alfred Lunt's eyes and saw only a stained terra cotta porous tile floor. Thursday morning I kept a taxi waiting while I bought a gigantic roll of bright blue vinyl linoleum which I lugged home and laboriously cemented over every inch of our two-hundred-year-old kitchen floor. It took two nights to do because I waited until Art left the apartment after dinner for his nightly rounds. I couldn't bear to hear what he'd have said if he'd seen me lifting heavy appliances, moving tables and chairs, cutting and pasting, perspiring and praying I'd finish the messy job in time.

Alfred Lunt arrived three hours early on the appointed Saturday morning. I was exhausted from working on my hands and knees halfway through the night before. Alfred brought along his own chef from the States, a jolly black man laden with utensils, who had taken the Cordon Bleu course alongside his boss. The atmosphere in our apartment was pure tension for twelve straight hours as Alfred and his sidekick prepared course after course, sending me off to far corners of Paris every hour or so for more supplies, another live lobster, no make that two, and a chicken, and a couple pounds of butter.

As our eight chosen guests arrived, one couple escorting Lynn Fontanne in an ethereal new Balmain caftan—she seemed to float above the entire evening—Alfred Lunt came over to where I was fussing with nonmatching wine glasses at the dinner table and said, "Y'know, I haven't had a drink in twenty years, but right now I'd like a good stiff Scotch." The nervous fear in his face, the perspiration shining on his handsome forehead had nothing to do with acting.

It was a turning point for me, and I joined the party.

But when VIPs departed, their eyes red from lack of sleep, we all returned to the simple entertaining we enjoyed, usually serve-yourself dinners in each other's houses where the kids answered the door and afterwards joined in the inevitable charades. For years we ended almost every evening divided into two fiercely competitive teams to play "the game." In time we invented so many esoteric and unfair signals that we finally had to give up; no one could remember them all.

When Art was away I spent most evenings with my American girlfriends. We'd meet for an early movie, go on to a small restaurant, then sit for hours at Fouquet's or Chez Alexandre's, wobbling home at 1:00 A.M., having talked over our problems and let our hair down. Dorothy Schoenbrun did it literally one night. Returning to their apartment very late, David went into their bathroom and gasped: on the top of the toilet tank, placed in perfect relationship to each other, were Dorothy's earrings, necklace, reading glasses, and new hairpiece. "My God," he wondered in panic, "did she flush the rest of herself away?"

Nights when Art went out with the boys were usually spent with the gang at Time-Life playing gin rummy with Dmitri Kessel and Frank White. Sometimes he would call me saying he had to work late. I'd hear the laughter in the background and know he was losing. When that happened he wouldn't stop playing until he either won or went broke.

Whenever Art won big we bought something we needed for the

house. We acquired our first washing machine with Art's winnings from Frank White. When Frank and his wife Drew came to visit the following week, we hung a big sign on the machine saying "The Frank White Memorial Washer." Refusing to even smile, Drew said, "That's thrilling. Now you'll have time to come watch me wash Frank's shorts by hand."

ART: **I know it sounds weird that with all the things we were doing and all the people we were entertaining we had time for Scrabble and gin rummy. One of the reasons I had time for gin rummy, which I played almost every afternoon, was that we ate dinner very late, usually at nine or ten o'clock.**

Life **photographers Gjon Mili, Dmitri Kessel, and Mark Kaufman and *Time* and *Life* editors Milt Orshefsky and Frank White were my favorite pigeons. We sat in Frank's office overlooking the Place de la Concorde, one of the most beautiful squares in the world, hunched over our cards for hours. Sometimes a call would come in from some poor helpless correspondent covering the Algerian war, and White, who was losing eighty dollars, would refuse to talk to him. Once Andrew Heiskell, now chairman of Time-Life, then a big-shot editor, walked in the office. I didn't look up or say anything. Heiskell was furious, stomped out and told someone to fire me.**

"We can't," the person said. "He doesn't work for us."

Another time I was involved in an afternoon gin game with Ben Bradlee who was then Paris correspondent for *Newsweek.* We were playing in my office when my secretary Ursula Naccache came in and said "There is a Congressman John Lindsay and his wife, who wish to see you."

"Tell them I'm in conference," I said, looking at my lousy hand.

Twenty minutes later Ursula said, "They're still out there."

I got up and went out to see them. I was still holding my cards.

Lindsay said, looking at the cards, "Sorry to break up the conference."

I figured I was dead anyway so I said, "I'm sorry—I was holding a jack and a king but I could never pick up the queen to go with it."

The Lindsays laughed, and when we moved to Washington they lived around the corner from us and to this day have remained friends.

From time to time our American friends invited each other over for dinners of typical, plain American dishes for which we were homesick. One Thanksgiving I worked three days, first locating, then stuffing and roasting a twenty-pound turkey (the French had nothing but disdain for anyone who'd bother with a fowl weighing more than two or three pounds), only to have Danielle, our maid, dissect it in the kitchen like leftover cold cuts.

For poker games we dashed across town to the only Kosher store in Paris for salami, pastrami, corned beef, and pickles. Ruth Ascarelli and I once announced that we would make chicken cacciatore for dinner. We'd learned how at the previous day's cooking school lesson. Working at fever pitch in her kitchen, the complicated recipe pinned to a curtain, I concocted my share of the dish following instructions for two people while Ruth happily quadrupled ingredients for her share—it was a watery disaster.

The best home-cooked dinners were at Hilda and George Marton's: Hungarian delights such as chicken paprika, Hungarian goulash, and roasted duck and goose. No one ever turned down an invitation to their apartment where twenty more guests would turn up for coffee and dessert. I remember meeting Mike Bessie and the Max Schusters, Sam Spiegel, and Irving Lazar at the Martons'. One afternoon Marjorie and Alain Bernheim summoned us to dinner with great excitement. A visitor had arrived by plane with a tray of smoked salmon and other specialties from the Stage Delicatessen in New York. We gathered around their kitchen table and ate with our hands.

In contrast to the wildly informal and hilarious parties given by our American friends, we were also invited, because of Art's job, to some of the most glamourous entertainments in Paris. The Duke and Duchess of Windsor were considered the greatest social catch in the city. The mere presence of the Duchess in the front row of a fashion opening assured the designer of a hit. Reporters and clients alike watched every movement of her hands. When she picked up the tiny gold pencil attached to her program and made a checkmark next to a model number, that particular dress, coat, or suit became the most newsworthy.

When we received a heavily engraved invitation to dinner at their town house near the bois de Boulogne, I spent three weeks making sure I would be properly dressed for the evening, and secure in the correct way to address the royal couple. He was still officially His Royal Highness, but though the British crown had denied the Duchess that title, the Duke apparently froze when anyone did not use it.

The evening of the party we called Jean, our building's maintenance man, who drove us when we were going further than a local taxi ride. He arrived at our door promptly, but announced that his car had broken down. "I have borrowed a 'peek-up' which is a little bit dirty on the outside but very clean where you sit." He and Art hoisted me up to the high cab, and I began to plead, "Art, don't let Jean drive us up to the door, please tell him to drop us off at the corner." Art said, "Not on your life. If the Duke needs us for dinner we can come any way we want. This is a very respectable van—what else could haul all those bricks?" He laughed, pointing through the back window to the flatbed truck heaped with a ton of building blocks.

We crunched onto the perfectly pebbled, curved driveway and

stopped smack in front of an open door where a butler was waiting. He looked at us, then at the van, trying to decide if we were at the wrong house.

I remember none of the other eighteen guests at the dinner table. I was too busy trying to learn how they ate the tiny pigeons. It turned out you had to chew up the tiny, fragile bones, which left me speechless for the rest of the meal. This was just as well since I was seated between two non-English-speaking Frenchmen. Dinner conversation in French always wiped me out.

I do remember vividly the beautiful living room—a glowing blend of gold, creamy white, and pale gray, lighted with dozens of tall, thin tapers in gold fixtures. Everyone looked glamorous in that room, even the men.

After dinner, the Duke put on one of his favorite recordings, a medley of patriotic German songs which startled his American guests into silence. Noting the lull, he switched to a new American record and said, "Let's all dance now!" Then he came over and, holding me at a three-foot distance, hurled me into an odd combination polka and waltz.

When the evening ended we bummed a ride home with a departing guest. Three days later we finally learned why we had been invited. "We would be so appreciative, Mr. Buchwald," the Duchess wrote, "if you let us know about any new restaurants you think we'd like—but none with garlic, please."

ART: **The thing that stands out when I recall the Duke of Windsor was his bursting into German song. He was a dimwitted man and I always believed England owes Wallis Windsor what's left of its empire for making him give up the crown.**

The Duchess, on the other hand, was a very sharp lady and knew what was going on. I wish I could say I went to their house because it was part of my job. But I'd be lying. I went there because I was fascinated with

this couple and all the swells that hung around them.

I suppose I had to sing for my supper because I was expected to say witty things about the members of the international set who weren't there that evening. Although Elsa Maxwell was purported to be the Duchess's best friend, she was always the patsy of the evening.

All the time we were in Paris I never quite stopped being awed by Europe's aristocracy or by the financial monarchs. One of my biggest moments as the "kid from Queens N.Y." was a night at the Palace Hotel bar in St. Moritz. It was one o'clock in the morning and sitting at my table were Gianni Agnelli of the Fiat company; Stavros Niarchos, the shipping billionaire; Fritz Opel, heir to the German automobile fortune; and Count Theo Rossi of Martini & Rossi vermouth. There were no wives present and the few girls in the bar would have nothing to do with any of us.

"I can't believe it," I told them. "There must be at least two billion dollars at this table, and not one of us can get lucky."

What attracted me to these people was that the men had power—more power than any businessmen in the United States. They could buy and sell heads of state (and did); they lived in their own world of pleasure and debauchery. Dope wasn't big in those days, so they pleasured themselves with lovers, mistresses, and trying to outwit and outspend each other.

Not all the people in the International Set had power. Some had titles and enough money to keep from getting into trouble by working. One Count I met spent his winters in St. Mortiz, his spring in Paris, London, and New York, his summer on the Riviera and his fall in Venice and Capri. He had been married four or five times. One

day he proudly showed me his watch and said "I have this watch cleaned every time I come to Switzerland. It doesn't lose one second from year to year.

"Why do you care?" I asked.

I ruined his holiday.

Another time at the Palace Hotel I played chess with a Spanish Duke whose name eludes me. He kept his set in the hotel safe and every afternoon at four we sat down in the card room to go at it.

One day he said, "I have a problem I wish to discuss with you?"

"Be my guest."

"It has to do with my hotel bill. Every time I get it they charge me 40 Swiss francs [$10] a day for my Schnauzer dog."

"That isn't out of line," I told him. "After all dogs tend to do things on carpets and chew up furniture."

"Yes," he replied. "I know that. But my dog has been dead for five years."

One of the most exciting extravaganzas in France was Aly Khan's annual dinner dance held every spring on the night of the Grand Prix. The Grand Prix was more than an international horse race; it was the social event of the year. Everyone attended, from the Premier of France and the English and European aristocracy to the stop-at-nothing starlets in picture hats and low-cut dresses. Afterwards Aly invited 200 guests to celebrate at the Pré-Catalan in the bois de Boulogne.

The word "charisma" was not popular in the fifties, but it certainly applied to Aly. Everyone liked him. Men admired his dashing skill at sports, and women adored him, including his ex-wives and those with whom he'd had a casual affair. The first year we met him I heard a story purporting to explain his sexual success. The Aga Khan, his father, believed that frequent sexual intercourse was the secret of mental and physical health. To insure his son's ability, he shipped the adolescent Aly to the same far-off guru he himself had visited to learn how to prolong the sex act and send women into ecstasy. True or false, Aly was known as a great lover. He had been married twice, once to Rita Hayworth, and his love affairs linked him to the most beautiful women in the world. One summer he had courted Gene Tierney who could not conceal her passion even in the company of her ever-present mother.

ART: **The trick was, Aly told me, to have two champagne buckets of ice—one on each side of the bed. Just before you felt you were about to ejaculate you were supposed to put your hands in the buckets. If you kept doing this you could stay in the saddle for hours and drive a woman mad.**

I've given a lot of thought to Aly's words and have even thought of investing in the champagne buckets. But if I had gotten too good at what Aly was supposed to be good at, I might have given up the column. Man cannot live by ice alone.

Art and I were invited to Aly's party for the first time about a year after we were married. Like every other woman I had a new dress made, but the moment we arrived, I knew mine had been a horrible mistake. I felt like a flower girl when I saw the slinky gowns around me. And perhaps because of my insecurity the evening quickly went from bad to worse.

We had arrived, by taxi, on the dot—which meant a half-hour early—to watch the flashy cars as they drove up. Aly had decorated the Pré-Catalan restaurant with flowers in his racing colors, hot pink and shamrock green. Set as it was among hundred-year-old trees and formal clipped hedges, the effect was overwhelming. The tables shone with silver and heavy lace, and at each place was a favor, not a simple party souvenir, but a toy from Cartier's or Van Cleef & Arpels.

Art stayed at my side only as long as it took to greet Aly and pick up a glass of champagne. Then, seeing someone he wanted to talk to, he wandered away saying, "I'll be right back." He did come back once, to show me to my table and to glance at the place cards on my right and left, whispering, "Boy, oh boy, are you going to have fun!" Both dinner partners turned out to be very old men from very old French families who talked about nothing but horse breeding. How I longed to be at Art's table where everyone seemed to be having fun.

When dinner was over, I waited for Art to come and take me into the next room to dance. Occasionally I heard his voice over the orchestra, but he was making no effort to look for me. As the music grew more frenzied and waiters began circulating with silver trays of champagne, I felt abandoned and inconsequential.

Finally I picked up my scarf from the chair where I'd left it and pretended to saunter self-confidently toward the ballroom, but instead of turning I kept right on walking, out the door, down the steps, and into one of the taxis lined up behind the shrubbery. On the long ride home I suddenly remembered that I had no money in my evening purse. When we drew up in front of our building, I said to the driver, "Wait a moment, please, while I get some money from my husband."

I went through every jacket Art owned, every pair of pants and all the junk on his dresser, finding a few francs at a time until I'd accumulated the equivalent of six dollars, five for the fare, one for a tip. I hadn't fooled the driver—he was dozing, his taxi meter turned off. He'd probably heard the "my husband" bit a thousand times.

Fifteen minutes later a wild creature stormed into the apartment. "What was that all about and what in hell are you doing *here?*"

ART: **It was two hours later.**

I tried a light touch. "Well, at least it's easier to find me in this tiny bathroom. . . ." But Art was furious. His evening had been spoiled. When my bathwater turned cold I toweled myself dry and we stalked each other through the apartment shouting insults at each other until we fell asleep exhausted around dawn, stiff back against stiff back.

ART: **Ann likes to think my evening was ruined. I had a wonderful time. I believe Aly knew more beautiful women in Europe than anyone during the fifties. He flirted with them, probably had flings with many of them, but his charm was such that even after he dumped a woman he remained on good terms with her. The ones who came to his parties were either ex-girlfriends or new ones. Aly was my kind of guy, and I fantasized that in the next world I would come back as the Aga Khan's eldest son.**

Aly's big party was an opportunity to meet a lot of people and I worked the open air garden, table hopping, ogling, and making many naughty mental notes.

I may not have paid enough attention to Ann, but I suspect she was uncomfortable in this crowd and frightened. Therefore when I didn't search for her after dinner she used my inattention as an excuse to go home.

Parties have always been a source of contention for us. I believe when you go to one, the purpose is to mingle with other people, even flirt innocently and have a good time. Ann thinks I should stick with her at a party. What's the sense of going to one if you spend the evenings talking to your wife?

We seem to always have a fight after a big party. Maybe it would be different if I had kept champagne buckets in the fridge on nights we went out.

We continued to go to Aly's parties until the last one in 1959—and gradually I overcame my original feelings of being the shortest, plainest, and only unaccomplished woman there.

Aly Khan died in the spring of 1960 as dramatically as he'd lived. Racing at top speed around a curve, he tried to dodge an oncoming car and crashed into a stone wall, throwing free his truest love, Bettina Graziani, but ending his own life. I wondered how many hundreds of women wept when they heard the news.

The weeks after Aly's parties were among the busiest in Paris, filled with dinners, dances and, it being June, weddings. Then in early July the city emptied out and most small businessess closed down. You could actually hear iron grilles clanging down over storefronts, heavy shutters scraping across entrances to be padlocked until the end of August.

For those who stayed behind, it was like living through a general strike. The law specified that one bakery, one dairy store, one grocery, one pharmacy be kept open in each quarter—in case people got hungry or sick—but finding the open ones was a nightmare. We thought the French were crazy to close up shop at the height of the tourist season, but they couldn't have cared less. They took two hours off for lunch, they often made love twice a day, to a mistress in the afternoon and a wife at night—so why not two months of vacation?

Art and I loved Paris best during those quiet sunny months. No traffic, no crowds on the Champs-Élysées—no taxis either, of course—no scrambling for sidewalk tables at the cafés, and plenty of time to entertain visitors.

That was all before we had children. Afterwards, we joined the general exodus to the beach and mountains. It's too bad our kids were so young. They only remember fragments of the best vacations they may ever have. Connie's clearest recollection of Switzerland is a massive bee sting. Joel recalls all the stops he made to be carsick. And Jenny talks most of the day I jumped, fully clothed, into a swimming pool to rescue her from drowning.

For family vacations we first went to Deauville, in Normandy, only three hours away from Paris by train. We stayed at the Hôtel Royal and every weekend droves of friends would arrive.

At night, Art and I would go to the Casino to watch the big-timers play. Some mornings the real diehards would still be sitting where we'd left them the night before, unshaven, unsmiling, praying to recoup. I was always struck by the little old ladies, often poorly dressed, who lined up around ten each morning waiting for the Casino doors to open.

I loved everything about Deauville (our house in Washington is as close as we could come to a Normandy country house) except the gambling, because I never won. Art would hand me $25 worth of chips and say "Go break the bank," but I hated throwing the equivalent of a new pair of shoes at strips of red and black felt. In addition, I'd been horrified by a story William Saroyan told me one night. He said he had gambled away his entire fortune. Two or three years before, rich from his best-selling books, he had sent his daughter off to college with the promise that she could spend the following summer with him in France. By May of the next year, she wrote that she was on her way, but he had to cable her not to come. "I didn't have enough money to rent even the cheapest room for her," he told me. Anatole Litvak, who'd made millions directing such film classics as *The Snake Pit*, was also said to have lost a fortune at the gambling tables. Saroyan kicked his addiction, but Litvak, like Darryl Zanuck and dozens of other Hollywood greats, never lost hope that someday they'd win back every dollar they'd lost.

One weekend I benefited from a big win myself. Herman Levin and his wife Dawn had arrived in Deauville, taking a short vacation from the Broadway show Herman was putting together for the fall. Late Saturday night Dawn and I grew weary of sitting alone at the Casino bar so we went back to our hotel rooms, leaving Art and Herman to gamble. The next morning I woke up early but Art was not there—his bed hadn't been slept in. A few minutes later he appeared, shaking his head as if he'd just walked away from a car crash, and handed me a small velvet jewelry box. "That was close, I'll tell ya," he sighed. "I almost lost my salary for the next two years, but I kept playing, winning a little, losing a lot, winning a lot, losing a little. Anyway I finally won a bundle and to be sure I'll never gamble again I spent it all at Van Cleef and Arpels . . . here." In the box was a pair of gold earrings set with the first real jewels I'd ever owned. Van Cleef stayed open twenty-four hours a day over the weekends so the big winners could reward their girlfriends for sitting beside them through the long nights.

I remember one other funny thing about that weekend. When Herman kept saying how excited he was about his play, Art told him to change the name. He didn't think *My Fair Lady* had enough zing.

ART: **I may have been right. If it wasn't for the book, the score and costumes, the cast and the lavish production, the show would have never worked. When I came to New York on a visit, Levin got me house seats to *My Fair Lady* at a time when tickets were impossible to get. It doesn't sound like a big deal now, but it was then. If you saw *My Fair Lady* during the first months of its opening your social status as a visitor to Manhattan was assured.**

One year we all went to Monte Carlo for a month. The "Blue Train" left Paris around seven in the evening, timed perfectly for a leisurely dinner in a dining car, and arrived in Monaco about eight o'clock the next morning. Art and I had a regular sleeping compartment next to a double for our nurse Kay and our three children, who spent the night drinking gallons of water so they could legitimately enjoy the most fascinating part of the trip, a concealed pull-down toilet which I heard them flipping in and out of the wall until dawn.

We rented one of the myriad cabanas on the beach and trundled down every morning in the Hermitage Hotel bus which ran fifteen-minute rounds between hotel and the shore. The children took swimming lessons while Art played gin rummy with anyone who wasn't sound asleep, and we ate off and on all day at our friends' cabanas. Some were so lavishly decorated with card rooms, bars, and sofas they seemed more like summer homes.

At night after we'd played with the children, Art and I would go to the Hôtel de Paris, to the Casino or the Sporting Club, or even better to boat parties. I'd never been aboard a private yacht and will always remember Stavros Niarchos's *Creole*. It was twilight and when we arrived an orange sun was sliding into the water. Orchestra music was coming from somewhere inside, and waiting to welcome us aboard was a slim and beautiful woman in a long dress of the palest green chiffon, the panels of her skirt drifting in the breeze. It was Niarchos's wife Eugenia for whose birthday the party was being given.

The *Creole*, a three masted sailing ship, had lush carpeting, crystal chandeliers, and incredible art. Van Gogh, Gauguin, and Monet hung in every stateroom. "Aren't paintings supposed to be kept away from water and dampness?" I asked Art.

"Stop worrying," Art whispered back. "If these peel off, Niarchos will go out and buy a new batch."

Onassis's yacht the *Christina* was just as lavish in its own way. It had a swimming pool which turned into a dance floor, two large motorboats and a seaplane. We went to another party on it a few nights later.

Betsy Grant, then Cary's wife, was one of the guests aboard that night. While we were having a drink she admired the barstools, which were shaped like tawny mushrooms. Ari sidled up and told her that they were made from one whale's penis. "Well, what do you know?" Betsy quipped. "Moby's dick."

ART: **The reader may get the impression that life for us was all gaming tables and Greek yachts. Actually, when we lived there, particularly in the late fifties, France was in turmoil and governments were falling left and right. De Gaulle came to power on this wave of anarchy and the right and the left were near civil war.**

There were serious riots on the Champs-Élysées and the place de la République. French riot police were out in force and if you weren't careful you could get hit by a cobblestone or policeman's blackjack. One evening

there was a big riot at the Rond-Point. Bob Yoakum was covering it for the *Trib* and came back to the office all bloodied.

"What happened?" we wanted to know.

"A flic (cop) came up to me and was about to club me. I told him I was an American reporter and showed him my French press card. He looked at it carefully, agreed I was—and hit me over the head."

The ultra-right, angry at what was happening in Algeria, resorted to placing bombs at their opponents' apartments. We would be in bed at the rue de Monceau and suddenly hear a loud explosion.

"What was that?" Ann asked.

"I believe someone is trying to blow up a Communist. Go back to sleep."

The only time I thought about pulling the entire family out of Paris was when the Four French Generals in Algeria took over the army there and threatened to invade the mainland. France's only other army was stationed in Germany and no one knew whom they were loyal to. De Gaulle stood between the Generals and civil war. It was his finest hour, and he went on radio and rallied the country. The French Generals in Germany remained faithful to him and the attempted overthrow failed.

But no one knew at the time how it was going to turn out. The reason I stayed was I felt that as the only American columnist in Paris I would look like a coward if I pulled out.

The night the paratroopers were supposed to have flown from Algiers to be dropped in Paris, I walked the streets of the city. Middle-aged men from the underground in World War II as well as Communists and socialists had gathered at the Grand Palais off the Champs-Élysées to enlist as a home guard. They were

issued everything but guns. I was frightened and I was sad. I was afraid the Paris I loved would be destroyed. Fortunately the attack never came and the back of the ultra-right wing in Paris was broken.

So it wasn't all fun and games. A bomb could go off anywhere. Once I was dining at the Berkeley, a great Paris restaurant, when a very loud explosion almost broke the windows. I rushed down to the rue du Faubourg St.-Honoré and saw a legless man lying in the street. The bomb, a plastique which looked like Silly Putty with a simple thermometer fuse, had been placed in a cake box a block from de Gaulle's palace. The poor man had been an innocent British tourist who was just walking by.

I only mention these things because Paris could be fun and also be dangerous. In those days, though, we had great faith in the American government and we thought foolishly that if anything happened they would be able to evacuate all of us. I only found out later that they were as confused as we were.

Our strangest vacations were the two summers we spent at Klosters in Switzerland. It was a small picturesque town where all the shops and even the main hotel were ornately trimmed with curlicued carved wood. It easily could have passed for paradise except for one problem: the Alps gave Art claustrophobia. Toward the end of our first week there, I woke up one morning to see him transfixed at the bedroom window. "This place gives me the creeps. Every morning when I look out I swear the mountains have moved in closer during the night. I'm going home for a few days."

So every Monday he took off for Paris, returning on Thursday for a long weekend. Guilt-ridden, he would immediately plan festive days of togetherness.

One weekend he said, "I've found an old farmer who'll rent us his horse and wagon—we'll take the kids on a hayride!"

"Do you know how to drive a horse and wagon?" I asked timidly.

"It's not something you have to learn, you do it," he answered.

That afternoon we piled the three children into the soft hay and, more as an afterthought than anything else, asked the farmer how to say Stop and Go in German. His answer seemed simple enough. But the horse had never heard accents like ours. As soon as Art picked up the reins, the horse veered off the main dirt road and headed up the mountain, at a graceful angle which tilted the wagon to a frightening degree. As the climb grew steeper and the horse's trot faster, the lower side of the wagon slanted to mere inches above the ground.

By the time we neared the top, I was sure we were going to crash. Only two of the wagon's wheels were touching the earth, the other two spinning in air. Art was hoarse from hollering at what might have been a deaf horse. Finally he turned to me and said, "Save the kids! Get 'em out of the wagon for God's sake. This thing is ready to fall!"

I crawled back from the driver's seat to the wagon where the children were crouching together, wondering when the fun was supposed to start. I gave Joel, then six years old, a stiff push and he leaped over the side like an antelope. Then I heaved Connie and Jenny out onto the prickly mountain grass. Jenny began crying even before her bottom hit, because she thought I was trying to get rid of her. "You threw me away and ripped my pants and I want to go back to Kay," she sobbed.

We waited helplessly on the mountainside for about an hour before a villager came by. He accepted a wad of money from Art and nodded that, yes, he would take the horse and wagon back to its owner. He gestured for us to climb aboard but we said "No thanks," which sounds the same in every language, and began picking our way down to safety.

ART: **The story is accurate in every detail. It taught me a big lesson and that was just because you can afford to rent a horse and wagon doesn't mean you can drive one.**

Had the horse not taken pity on me I don't think I'd be here to make these comments today.

To this moment I have nightmares of Ann in black sitting somewhere on a porch and a lady saying, "How did your husband die?" and she replies, "He was driving a horse and wagon in Switzerland and he instructed the horse to take him right over a cliff."

One of the most valuable trips the children went on was back to the States to receive American citizenship. Like many Americans living abroad who had adopted babies from different countries, the question of citizenship haunted us. United States law required three years' residence in the U.S., but how could the five of us spend all that time in the States? Art's career would have gone down the drain. And you can't send a trio of toddlers across the ocean, saying, "Just keep busy . . . time will go fast . . . before you know it, you'll be Americans."

In the fall of 1958, thanks to a concerted effort in which Art played a part, the American government had okayed a temporary exemption for children under seven years of age; they could become citizens after thirty days in the United States. The exemption would stay in effect for two years only.

Art and I rejoiced and acted fast. Then we flew to New York and rented a suite at a residential hotel in New York, borrowing everything we needed for the kitchen from our friends Hansi and Terry Cline. Joel was five; Connie, three; and Jennifer, two. My mother came from Warren to help.

On December 30, the morning they were sworn in, we dressed the children meticulously. You'd have thought they were planning to report in to the President of the United States as soon as they'd been made citizens. I still have a picture of them sitting on the steps of the Federal Court in lower Manhattan. A large American flag is draped across their laps and they are saluting like soldiers.

Inside the courtroom, we realized that ours were the only children present. We stood in a solemn row. My mother's eyes nervously watched for any signs of misbehavior while Art's father seemed overwhelmed by memories of his own naturalization fifty years earlier.

As the judge finished his welcoming speech, Jenny wriggled out of my mother's grasp and began creeping from rung to rung under the tunnel of locked-together chairs. "Quick, pick up that baby, that floor is FILTHY!" my mother whispered. Her final word unfortunately fell into a small pool of silence. All eyes dropped to inspect the floor.

For the rest of the ceremony we managed to avoid further interruptions. Connie looked as if she were hanging on the judge's every word, but she was actually waiting for him to finish. She had asked me where the bathroom was and I'd promised, "As soon as the man stops talking, we'll go find it." Only Joel sensed that something out of the ordinary was taking place and made a good stab at the words in the oath, especially at the end when he said, "avec liberty et justice for everybody."

The entire process which transformed our children into American citizens took only a few minutes and was in some ways as anticlimactic as being married by a distracted justice of the peace. But Art and I knew we could finally stop worrying. The children would never have to serve any country but our own.

ART: **Joe McCarthy's influence still hung over the country and every alien had to swear he wasn't a Communist or had ever been one. Since the kids were too young, I had to swear for them. I told Ann "I swore for them. I'm glad they didn't ask me if I had been one because I would have refused to answer."**

Once we left Paris and came to live in Washington all three children adapted to American life with lightning speed, refusing to spend time remembering the past. For years they refused to discuss visiting Paris. Any mention of taking them to look at the countries of their birth provoked stony silences, emphatic "No thanks," or sometimes "What a yucky idea!" It seemed strange to me. Most of their friends would have given anything to go on one of the European school tours. But not our kids—they left the room whenever we brought up the subject.

Then, surprisingly, one day in 1972 Art and I asked Connie if she'd like to go to Spain with us and she said yes. We flew to Madrid in early June, and immediately we found Conchita, Connie's godmother who had helped us survive the tortuous Spanish adoption laws sixteen years before. Together we explored the city until Connie was not only at ease but in love with Spain. Then Art and I took her to see the hospital where we had found her.

It was just as we'd remembered: spotlessly clean, its walls covered with hand-painted tiles, its corridors buzzing with scurrying nuns. We went straight up to the nursery on the second floor where the newborn babies still slept in two long rows of white metal cribs. Wordlessly, we walked from one bed to another. It was Connie who spoke first: "I'm glad I came from here," she said. Art and I just looked at each other with tears in our eyes.

With the tension broken, Connie and I began arguing about which baby was the prettiest—"My Jesúsa is much more beautiful than that skinny little José you like"—joking about how we'd steal the best of the bunch and take it home with us. A nun with a puckish face sensed what we were saying and though she couldn't speak English she pattered over to me and in pantomime suggested that I quickly tuck one of the babies under my skirt—and run!

It was Connie who helped Art and me accept how difficult it is for adopted children to contemplate their beginnings. "Y'know," she said one afternoon a couple of months after we'd returned from Spain, "I used to dream about what my natural mother was like; I always imagined she would be someone perfect and wonderful and beautiful. When I got mad I'd secretly plan to run away and find her. Now I don't like her at all. She shouldn't have left me all alone when I was only five days old. I don't dream about her anymore."

That was a breakthrough. Now we hope that Joel and Jenny will soon lay their ghosts to rest. I have a hunch it won't be long before they do. Earlier this year Jenny, having graduated from Emerson College, said she was considering going to Paris to enroll in a new French cooking school. And even as I write I'm aware that Joel, who works for ABC News, is on a TWA plane flying to Paris and England, "And," he added on the phone last night, "maybe I'll go to Ireland, I'm not sure yet. . . ."

Seven

Life with Art meant constant travel and some of my best memories of those years abroad were the times I packed up to cover an assignment with him. One of our first trips together was in November of 1955, just as Paris became its coldest and most depressing.

Art woke me up at one o'clock in the morning with a call from Naples where he'd gone to do a series on Lucky Luciano. If I could organize myself quickly I could meet him in Vienna that weekend for the reopening of the Opera House. The Vienna State Opera had been closed for ten years and all Austria was awaiting the first performance since the war. They'd invited George London—who'd flown from the States weeks in advance—to sing *Fidelio*.

It was a fabulous weekend. During the day we ate mountains of pastries, gawked at castles, oohed at the Danube, and I went to Mass at St. Stephen's. The cathedral was so ancient and Gothic that I told Art, "If I'd gone to a church like this when I was a child I'd be in a convent by now."

In the afternoon we visited Schönbrunn Palace and sent David and Dorothy a card saying, "You'd better get here quick, they're misspelling your name." We also visited the Lipizzaner horses, famous for their dancing exhibitions.

That night as we dressed for the opening, I worried about everything: my clothes, my hair, what I would say to dignitaries. It was the first time I'd seen Art in white tie and tails. He'd rented everything except socks and it took us two hours to dress him properly.

It's odd that after all the grandeur, my most vivid memory is the moment when all the lights came on after the opera. I turned to John Crosby, the New York *Herald Tribune* television critic, who was seated on my right. He had fallen asleep with his head snuggled into the curve of an elegant woman's neck, a stranger in a strapless ball gown who was sitting motionless either out of embarrassment or motherliness. She hadn't dared lift her hands to applaud. I roused John, who rubbed his eyes and asked, "How do you like it so far?"

ART: **The trip to Naples, which Ann skipped over lightly so she could get to Vienna, was far more interesting for me than the opening of the Vienna Opera House.**

It originated one day in Paris when a deported gangster from the U.S. came in to see Ben Bradlee at *Newsweek*. Bradlee, a bosom pal then as now (I was best man at two of his weddings), wanted nothing to do with Frank Frigenti, a man who carried newspaper clippings of his crimes in his wallet. What Frigenti was doing was trying to peddle a story on Italians who had been sent back to Naples by the U.S. immigration officials. Frigenti, for a price, would reveal how they were operating in white slavery, drugs, and what-not. The most famous of these was Lucky Luciano. The rest were second- and third-rate gangsters with minor league reputations. Bradlee thought it would be a big joke to turn Frigenti over to me since *Newsweek* wasn't interested.

He brought the ex-con down and introduced him.

Frigenti wanted $1000 to tell his story. I offered him $20 and he took it. I could not be accused of checkbook journalism because I paid him in cash.

It turned out Frigenti told a hair-raising story of intrigue and crime along the Naples docks. It made a very good column particularly since I didn't bother to check any of it out.

A few weeks later I received a letter from five deportees living in Naples telling me Frigenti was a liar and inviting me to Naples to see what a sad life they lived.

I went down, and except for Luciano, who had a penthouse and was being well taken care of by the mob in the U.S., the other deportees were indeed in bad shape. The Italian gangsters would have nothing to do with them because they were being so closely watched by the Neapolitan police. Although they were born in Italy, many had come to the United States when they were very young and considered themselves Americans. To survive they were forced to pull petty con games against the tourists, including short changing lire for dollars and selling fake Parker fountain pens made in the back alleys of the city.

I got a crook's tour of Naples and a series of pieces including an exclusive interview with Luciano.

Luciano took me to a restaurant overlooking the Bay of Naples. Before seeing him I had bought a coral necklace for Ann in a shop for $100. During lunch I showed him the necklace and asked him if I had been cheated. He called over a man from another table and asked him to examine it.

"How much did you pay?" the man asked.

"One hundred dollars."

The man said to Luciano "Whoever sold him this necklace should be shot."

"Goddamnit," I said.

Luciano looked at me and said, "Watcha' complaining about? These Wops do this to me every day."

The reason the trip was so productive was I decided to write a novel about a deportee who was sent back to Italy and got screwed by the Italians in much the same manner he had been screwing everyone in the U.S. It was titled *A Gift from the Boys*—the gift was a girl the mob gave him as a going-away present. Cary Grant read the book in galleys and indicated he wanted to play the deportee. Stanley Donen, the director, heard this and told Irving Lazar, the agent, he wanted the book. Lazar sold it him for $50,000, which to me was a windfall of money.

Unfortunately Donen botched the script; Grant decided it wasn't my story, which was true, and turned it down. A year later Donen sold Yul Brynner on making it, not in Sicily, where the story took place, but in Greece. It was renamed *Surprise Package* and was one of the great clinkers of the year.

But I did make $60,000 between the book sales and the movie deal, so I couldn't complain. Bradlee, to this day, insists he should have gotten half for introducing me to Frigenti.

It was rather interesting to go from the dregs of the American underworld in Naples to the white tie opening of the Vienna Opera House. It was quite a sentimental occasion, but I had mixed feelings about it. I thought to myself at the time, the same people who were shedding tears for their opera house were the first ones to greet Adolf Hitler with open arms, and alas, George London, an American Jew, had been given the honor of singing *Fidelio* at this historic moment.

* * *

Many of the trips I took with Art were financed by Conrad Hilton. Whenever he invited Art to cover the opening of one of his hotels, I was always guaranteed a ticket. In 1959 we went to Cairo so Art could report on the new Nile Hilton.

We left Paris on a cold rainy day in February, waiting two hours for the fog to lift for our flight to Italy, two more hours in Rome for our flight to Athens, and a final two hours in Greece for no apparent reason before going on to Egypt. It was the first time Art had dared enter an Arab country, but his passport was stamped without question.

The Nile Hilton was by far the most beautiful hotel Conrad had built. Our room overlooked the famous river and the view was magnificent. The only drawback was that the workmen were not quite finished. The lobby was mostly wet plaster, only partially trimmed with specially designed mosaic tiles; the elevators still didn't work; and bathroom doors were stacked at the end of the halls.

A charter plane came in from the States the day after we did, loaded with stars to celebrate the opening. Among them were Edie and Van Johnson, Mary and Bob Cummings, Jane Russell, Sonja Henie, Martha Hyer, Hugh O'Brian, Jeanne Crain and her husband, Ann Miller and husband Bill Moss, Leonard and Sylvia Lyons, Governor and Mrs. Earl Warren, and of course Conrad himself.

We rode down the Nile, or up—I have never understood which way it flowed—on a beautiful yacht that had once belonged to King Farouk and his father. As we ate the exotic food and listened to soft Eastern music we gossiped about King Farouk's orgies which had led people to call the ship the *Pleasure Boat.*

One morning we all went to Ghiza and spent hours photographing each other in front of the pyramids and the Sphinx. Afterwards we were shown a mile-deep chasm where archeologists had been working for five years to unearth their most recent discovery, the Solar Boat, a huge wooden ship perfectly preserved for 5,000 years in the dry Egyptian sand. The ancient Egyptians had built the boat in the solemn belief that when they died it would carry them to the sun for eternity. It was primitive but fully equipped with masts and dozens of heavy oars. Hoping to discover an ancient souvenir on my own, I spent hours jamming my shoes into the sand until I found what looked like a piece of rare amber, smooth and gold-tinted. Our guide laughed; it was part of a local beer bottle.

In the evenings we were entertained on rooftop terraces, in palaces, and at lavish dinners by belly dancers who entranced our husbands. Even Marshal Tito arrived from Yugoslavia to surprise Nasser on the first anniversary of the United Arab Republic. Art went to Revolution Square to hear him speak to the screaming masses.

The highlight of the trip was the Tutankhamen collection on exhibit in Egypt twenty years before anyone thought of bringing it to the United States. An eager young curator named Pepsi welcomed a handful of us early one morning and casually led us from case to case where the boy king's priceless belongings were displayed in ordinary wood and glass cabinets like those used in old department stores. All the doors were unlocked, and since the exhibits were poorly lighted, Pepsi invited us to pick up anything we wanted to look at closely. I wandered around with a small, exquisite teacup and saucer, each piece carved from a single, gigantic emerald, until I located Art to show him its translucent greenness.

When I think of the millions of Americans who had to stand behind velvet ropes and "keep moving" when the King Tut exhibit traveled across the United States, I can't believe the nonchalance with which we browsed.

ART: **The museum was in such disrepair and so badly run that countless treasures were stolen over the years. They were sold to museums in other countries who asked no questions of how they got out of Eygpt.**

Sonja Henie, the retired ice-skating movie queen, was in our group and jewels were her passion. I remember that she was wearing a fortune in diamonds that morning, despite the early hour. Whenever she spied an especially spectacular object, she whipped a jeweler's loupe from her purse and popped it in her eye.

After we'd seen the treasures, Pepsi beckoned us to follow him down to a cavernous room under the museum where we were surrounded by walls of tombs and rows of mummies, some in and others out of their ancient sarcophagi. Pepsi identified the bodies as wives, mistresses, children, pets, and even a few faithful servants who had been buried alive with their dead masters.

ART: **The Hilton and Sheraton junkets served a very useful purpose. It gave me an opportunity to take Ann with me in style. Also because of being Jewish, it was the only way I could get into Egypt.**

One night I was standing in the hotel lobby alone and a priest came up and asked me to speak to the students at the American University in Cairo. He didn't know I was Jewish and I thought it would be fun to do it.

The next day I stood up in front of 2000 Egyptian students and pleaded with them not to burn down the new Hilton Hotel (they had recently burned Shepheard's Hotel to the ground during a riot) because, while it was named Hilton, it was actually owned by Egyptians.

The other thing I remember was that the Egyptian staff for the hotel were not too well trained. I sent my tuxedo down to be pressed and my shoes to be shined in the morning.

At six I called the valet. The tux he said was on its way. At seven it was still on its way. At eight I got angry and yelled, "Not only don't I have my tuxedo, but I don't have my shoes."

The valet asked, "What do you need your shoes for if you don't have your suit?"

But the junkets paid off. We got to exotic places and

after a trip together Ann didn't complain about me being away from home for at least a month.

One of our gayest trips turned out to be our last fling in Europe, but neither Art nor I had any inkling of the fact at the time. Art had been in Cannes for a week, covering an international convention of travel agents. It was our eighth wedding anniversary and I was longing to be with him when he called to say, "Why don't you meet me in Rome? We'll go see how Liz is doing."

Two major American films were being made in Rome that fall, the extravaganza *Cleopatra* with Elizabeth Taylor, Richard Burton, and Edward G. Robinson; and *Two Weeks in Another Town*, based on Irwin Shaw's novel, starring Cyd Charisse and Kirk Douglas. *Cleopatra* was in financial trouble; it had already gone over its multimillion-dollar budget and wasn't half-finished. Elizabeth had had frequent bouts of illness and there were rumors the film would never be completed.

But when I arrived at the Excelsior to meet Art I didn't notice a single negative vibration. The hotel lobby was a crush of familiar faces. For a moment I wondered if everyone we'd ever met had suddenly moved to Rome!

It was a wonderful, light-hearted week. I can still remember the warm sun on my back and feel the soft breezes which played with the fringed umbrellas along the Via Veneto. The men were outrageously handsome, with their unbuttoned shirts billowing open to reveal bronzed chests. They would drift from table to table in the cafés, flirting with one pretty girl after another, arranging their love lives for the night ahead. In the mornings I would leave Art asleep to go sightseeing. I was afraid to miss anything.

One day Frank Folsom, an American RCA executive, told Art he'd arranged a private audience for us with the Pope. Frank was very specific about the protocol involved. He would pick us up at 9:00 the following morning and would personally escort us through the Vatican. The afternoon he invited us, I scoured Rome for an appropriate black dress and veil while Art ran around buying rosaries and religious medals. He returned to the hotel with dozens which my family still treasures today.

"How did you know to choose this?" I asked, holding up a Miraculous medal.

"Oh, it just looked kind of pretty," he said.

The next morning Art and I were waiting in the lobby an hour ahead of time, and as we drove to the Vatican I kept rehearsing exactly what I should do and say. On our arrival we were led into a small, ornate room and told to wait. Art whispered, "Talk about private . . . this must be the smallest room in the Vatican." We were thrilled at the prospect of being so close to the Pontiff. A few minutes later, the door opened and we were beckoned by a Vatican guard to a different room, this one somewhat larger but just as empty as the first one. Several more minutes passed and we were escorted to a third, vast hall, the largest in the Vatican. As we gazed around in awe, we saw thousands of people coming to join us—troops of Boy Scouts, military units, marching bands, schools, whole villages. Eventually 8,000 people crammed into the hall, crushing us against the wall as a path was cleared for the entrance of Pope John XXIII. He was seated on a plain wooden chair which was borne over the heads of the crowd, who chanted, "Papa! Papa! Papa!" I couldn't see a thing until two tall strangers made a chair with their hands and hoisted me up to a series of ledges, indicating where I should place each foot and hand. I wrote my mother: "I received the Papal blessing hanging by my fingernails—it counts double that way."

ART: **It may not have been the private audience we expected but it was more exciting. Pope John was in a class by himself and I never felt as moved as I was by a man in that vast hall. I have had few heroes in my time but he was one of them.**

When Art and I visited Elizabeth and Eddie Fisher we saw no signs of the impending scandal which was to wreck their marriage. They had rented a small but elegant villa chosen for its protective fringe of olive trees. The Fishers thought the trees would insure privacy from the insatiable Italian paparazzi but instead the branches provided fine nesting places for the photographers.

Like many Americans living temporarily in Rome, Elizabeth and Eddie went to restaurants and nightclubs almost every night, staying out until three or four in the morning. Then they slept until one or two o'clock in the afternoon. On the afternoon we arrived they were having champagne and eating breakfast, snuggled together at one end of a sofa, still dressed in their robes and pajamas and ostensibly as happy as clams.

We accompanied them to countless parties given by Kurt Frings, Elizabeth's agent, Sam Spiegel, Denise and Vincente Minnelli, and the Edward G. Robinsons in deceptively homelike bistros.

One night Tony Martin, then and still married to Cyd Charisse, and Eddie Fisher put napkins over their arms and pretended to be singing waiters. At the first table they approached were Italy's four greatest opera stars, who drowned them out, and sent them creeping back to our table. Another night Eddie Fisher, at Elizabeth's request, sang with the orchestra for nearly two hours. When we left at 4:00 A.M. the remaining diners resumed eating and dancing as if it were early evening.

The next day we visited the set of *Cleopatra*, where the Forum had been recreated down to the last monumental detail. We lounged and ate sandwiches in one of Elizabeth's four dressing rooms (one was reserved just for her wigs!). The whole time Eddie never moved from her side. They were waiting for the director to call her for a big scene they had been rehearsing for days. Cleopatra was to enter the gates of the Forum atop a giant golden Sphinx, where she would rise from her peacock throne and dramatically descend the golden steps to approach Burton. Walter Wanger, the producer, had offered me a part as an extra that morning, but when Art heard my enthusiastic acceptance he yelled, "Don't be ridiculous! You'll just have to stand around in rags waiting for him to yell 'Peasants in place!' " I later thanked Art for saving me since extras kept fainting during the endless hours, standing idle in the hot sun.

Finally, as the daylight faded, filming began. The mighty gates opened and in rolled the golden Sphinx, propelled by Cleopatra's slaves. Elizabeth rose from her throne and with dazzling beauty and majesty began her slow descent. Halfway down the narrow steps she stopped, and with one hand on her head, the other covering her mouth, cried, "I just can't do it, I'm so dizzy I can't move, someone come and get me!" That was that for the day. We all went back to her dressing rooms and had more champagne.

When we returned to Paris we were shocked to hear that Elizabeth's marriage was on the rocks. "Not true at all," we kept telling our friends. "We've just come back from Rome and we saw the Fishers every day; they're completely happy." But before the week was over, every Paris newspaper carried banner headlines proclaiming "Liz and Burton in Love" . . . "Cleopatra and Caesar are for Real" . . . "Liz and Eddie Call it Quits." I have no idea whether Sybil Burton saw the romance budding, but I suspect Eddie Fisher was every bit as surprised as we were.

ART: **They called Rome in those days "Hollywood on the Tiber." Eddie was Mike Todd's best friend. Eddie tried to be, but he never was, Mike Todd. It was inevitable that the marriage wouldn't last. But I never looked for gossip for my column so I never knew what was going on. I just assumed everyone in Europe was fooling around with somebody. Only after it became a fact did I use the gossip to write a funny column.**

Since people knew that gossip wasn't my bag most of them felt safe in my company and never had to worry about me violating a confidence. But I'm not against gossip. In fact, I have always believed scandal serves a very useful place in our civilization. People can't deal with cold wars and threats of nuclear destruction. But they love to read about well-known people in trouble. It makes them feel better. Most of those I know who condemn the diet of scandal in our daily newspapers eat up

every word. I know when I went back to the United States everyone I met was far more interested in what was going on with Ingrid Bergman and Roberto Rossellini, than when the next Italian government would fall.

***Cleopatra* was a multimillion-dollar disaster when it was being made, and the Taylor-Burton romance added more scandal to the film. But the horror of it all was that it made people all over the world very happy.**

I don't know one major scandal that didn't bring joy to everyone except the people who were involved. In order to save our sanity we must have one every three months. In those days Rome produced its share, for which we all should be very grateful.

Art took several trips on which I would have gone only if I'd been forced into the trunk of his car. His most outrageous episode was driving to Russia from Paris in April of 1958 with Peter Stone. Neither had anything intriguing to do that month and so they decided that it was time to show the Communists how a couple of Capitalists lived.

They made a handsome deal with the head of Chrysler in Europe, a Mr. Armstrong, who recognized the publicity value of the articles Art would write about motoring to Moscow. He lent them a new Chrysler Imperial and paid for its chauffeur, a Belgian in full livery.

A few days before Easter they loaded up the car with a tub of chocolate chip cookies for themselves; and jars of cheap French caviar and Western work-savers such as a battery-powered boot scraper and squeegee mops for the Russians.

They pulled out of Paris at dawn and drove first to Munich, then on to Vienna, then to Warsaw, arriving in that Catholic city on Easter Sunday. There were all-night parties and dancing in the streets. It took them seven days and seven nights to get to Moscow where Art cabled, REACHED RUSSIA THIS MORNING BUT STILL LOVE BOURGEOIS YOU.

On their way they lost their movie camera; Art left it on the hood of a farmer's truck. Several times they lost control of the Chrysler in snowdrifts so deep that peasants had to form human chains to tug them out. And twice they almost lost their freedom. The first time Art unwittingly photographed military installations as they crossed the border into Russia. The second escapade was deliberate. He and Peter stuck two American flags on the Chrysler and crashed a Communist Party Rally at the Sports Palace where Khrushchev was the speaker. The KGB assumed they had been invited and gave them the best box in the house.

ART: **The Russian trip was the type of thing that worked very well. I was Walter Mitty and the readers went along for the ride.**

The Russian people were very friendly though the officials were stiff and nervous. My articles have been used in the Soviet press for thirty years. They usually pick the ones that attack the U.S. government. When I was in Moscow in 1958 I asked the editor at *Izvestia* "Since you always print my pieces when I attack the U.S., will you run any of my articles where I make fun of the Soviet Union?"

He said with a straight face "We don't have the space."

I got ten pieces out of the Russian trip though Chrysler was somewhat miffed because I had taken a photograph which was printed with one article showing a horse pulling the Chrysler out of the snow in Poland. The caption read "One more horse added to a Chrysler engine."

Three weeks after they drove off, Art and Peter returned to Paris by plane. Peter's mother, Hilda Marton, and I didn't recognize them when we met them at Orly. They looked like escapees from a work camp, bearded and wearing earmuff caps and heavy jackets lined with what looked like dog fur. Art handed me my present in the car, a crude white tablecloth hand-embroidered in garish colors. "You'd better like it," he said. "In rubles it cost $400; there isn't a husband in Russia who could afford one. You're just plain lucky."

Sometimes, despite all the excitement of living abroad, my longing for my family became overwhelming. But we never talked about homesickness. We knew there was no point. Throughout our Paris years I can't recall hearing any American openly admit to being homesick and to this day I can't translate the phrase into French.

Yet the condition was always there. The two words "home" and "Paris" were never interchanged. When we said we were going home, I meant Warren, Pennsylvania, and Art meant Forest Hills, New York. When we referred to where we actually lived, where our apartment was, where our jobs, hopes, hearts, and children were, we'd say, "We have to go *back*." "Back" was Paris. Whenever I was traveling my diary notes, "All OK in Paris." Paris was a city with a capital "P." Home was a noun which it was improper to mention with real emotion.

Periodically I would drag myself to see Dr. Paul-Émile Seidman or Dr. John Dax and submit my symptoms: insomnia, no energy, crying spells. No one ever said, "You are homesick." Instead the doctors would prescribe vitamin shots, fewer nights on the town, or a reminder to drink red wine only—white was toxic for women. There was no medication for a recurring ache to eat homemade cinnamon buns in my mother's kitchen, to touch everyone sitting around the table, or to hear my grandmother say over and over, "For land's sake!"

Conrad Hilton cured my most acute case of homesickness when Joel was just twenty months old. I had been dying to show the baby to my family but Art did not foresee a trip to the States before the end of the year. Suddenly, at the close of a lavish weekend in Turkey where Art and I had been part of the invited press group celebrating the opening of a new Hilton Hotel in Istanbul, Mr. Hilton announced that there were going to be a few empty seats on his charter plane returning to New York. Several guests had decided that as long as they were halfway around the world, they might as well explore the rest of the Middle East. "If any of you want a free ride back to the States, you can have it, providing you don't break quarantine. That means you have to stay on the airplane from the time it leaves Istanbul until it lands in New York."

I could go home! And our friend Dick Barkle who was in Istanbul but not on the charter agreed to bring Joel to New York on a Pan Am flight leaving just seven hours after mine.

Everything went on schedule. The charter plane arrived at Orly at noon, and I stayed on it. Art scurried off, relieving me of all my luggage except for a small overnight case. I would wait for Joel in New York.

I don't know how Art managed to obtain a temporary visa for Joel at the American Embassy in just seven hectic hours, nor how he explained to a puzzled Nanny that her charge was going to fly to the United States in the arms of a stranger. He told me later that she went into a state of shock. Art had to dress Joel himself and do all the baby's packing, getting step-by-step instructions over the phone from Ruth Ascarelli, who told him how many diapers, shirts, sweaters, etc., to include. For good measure Art also added Joel's potty, along with toys, vitamins, a snowsuit, and twenty-four jars of Gerber's baby food.

Art cabled his family to meet me at the Waldorf, and wired my mother that Joel and I would be arriving in twenty-four hours. He reserved two seats for us on an Allegheny Airlines flight out of New York. Then with Joel, Barkle, visa, and enough luggage for a trip around the world, he rushed back to Orly in time for Barkle and the baby to board the 7:00 P.M. Pan Am plane for New York. Worn out, he went back to the apartment and gave Nanny ten days off so he wouldn't have to explain what had happened.

I remember smiling to myself as I flew toward New York. I was traveling with one dress, one nightie, a bunch of lipsticks, and some makeup for my first visit home in two years. Thank heaven for J. C. Penney, I thought. And for plenty of sisters who wore the same size clothes.

The next morning I was out on the runway, standing at the bottom of the steps when the plane landed. The first passenger to disembark was an exhausted Barkle, carrying a pink-cheeked, wide-eyed baby who was as serene as if he'd just been lifted out of his crib. Neither of them had closed their eyes during the fourteen-hour flight. "He was terrific!" Barkle shouted halfway down the steps. "He ate EVERYTHING!"

I found out exactly what he'd eaten as our small, nonpressurized Allegheny plane zoomed up and down for local stops on the flight to Warren. Joel vomited all the way.

A distinguished man wearing an expensive gray summer suit was sitting in the front seat across the aisle from us reading *The Wall Street Journal*. Every time Joel vomited, the man vomited. I could hear him gag and rattle the airsick bag discreetly behind his newspaper. I felt so sorry for what we were doing to him that I almost offered to hold his head, too.

By the time we landed in Jamestown, I'd used up all the clean diapers and baby garments in the emergency travel bag. We were a mess of tears and strained vegetables. I finally hired a taxi for the twenty-two-mile trip to Warren. The driver couldn't believe his luck. He muttered all the way, "Bus woulda come along in twenny, twenny-five minutes . . . most folks take the bus . . . goes faster'n this old crate I tell you . . . pulls up right there by the airport road. . . ." I wanted to scream, "We didn't have twenty-five minutes of clothes left." As if to excuse my extravagance, Joel kept vomiting.

I wasn't at all prepared for the emotional impact of returning to my home town after five years in Paris. When we hit the outskirts of Warren, I began to feel dizzy and lightheaded. Memories buzzed and flitted and banged into each other in my brain. The joy of knowing that in a few seconds I would be able to look at my family again, hug them, talk to them, was shadowed by a creepy fear: How had I managed to get out of this town? And Paris, was it real or only a dream? Would I truly be going back at the end of the week? I felt suspended between two worlds, my childhood and my life with Art in France. At that moment I treasured every facet of our marriage and longed for Art as though I'd been brutally torn from him. Yet as we drove up the newly paved road to my mother's house, and when I saw her and all my brothers and sisters bunched together on the tiny front porch, waving frantically as if they feared I might drive past the house, I began to cry. The tears were in gratitude. I'd come full circle; I was home again, everybody looked the same, nothing had changed—except me. For all the good things that had happened to me I felt I owed the town, that house, that family a lot. I began making mental lists of interesting people and events to tell my family; but first I would show them my wedding ring and our new son.

Determined not to present our pride and joy dressed as though he'd been playing in vegetable soup, I stripped Joel naked as we approached my mother's house. When we turned into the driveway, my whole family was grouped on the front lawn, waiting. I paid the driver, tossed our duffel bags onto the grass, and walked up to kiss my mother—carrying a baby as naked as the day he was born. "Here's your newest grandchild!" I shouted.

I was at last a valid member of the McGarry tribe, married, a mother, with a carsick baby to prove it. If they feared that we might be different, coming from France by way of Turkey, we certainly had arranged to look like everybody else who'd come home to that old house, dirty laundry and all.

Istanbul, the belly dancers, and sweet shops were too exotic to interest my family until I showed them the gold ring Art had bought me just before we left. It was an elegant version of the traditional Turkish wedding ring: five separate gold bands, each set with a different gem signifying happiness, health, wealth, long life, and many children. Art had surprised me with it. "Here," he'd said gruffly, "this makes up for the engagement ring I took back!" It was far more beautiful and fascinating.

To sit in the summer sun under the picnic tree at home, to smell my grandmother's moss roses, which wafted her back from heaven as clearly as if she'd come out of the kitchen with a batch of sugar cookies, to watch our baby toddle barefoot through real grass for the first time in his life, was the best cure for homesickness anyone ever had.

"Our Joel is the most loved baby in this family," I wrote Art. "Even my sisters who have beauties of their own rave about him."

Until my mother actually held Joel in her arms I'd been worried about how she would take to an adopted baby. But I'd overlooked one factor. Joel was 100 percent Irish, which only one other person in my mother's life had been able to claim: my father. Mom never said how much she missed that Irish husband of hers—we knew only that she trudged up to the cemetery to visit his grave every day of her life—but Joel had a special spot in her heart from the moment she saw him.

Although we continued to live in Paris for almost eight more years, I never again suffered seriously from homesickness. That trip home had shown me that the ties with my family were unbreakable.

Eight

Gradually we all began to drift back to the United States. Jobs grew into permanent careers. Foreign correspondents became editors in America. Children reached the age where, if they were to eventually live in America, they had to be educated in schools where English wasn't the second language. Writers, after years of struggling, suddenly saw their books on the New York *Times* best-seller list and were called home to publicize them, then stayed to enjoy their new celebrity status.

We hadn't even thought of moving back when a lecture bureau offered Art a fat fee to do a series of speaking engagements in the States late in January of 1962. It was too good to pass up. We took the children out of kindergarten, first and second grades, and flew directly to my mother's house in Warren, Pennsylvania, where I enrolled Joel in the local grammar school ignoring the fact that he could neither write nor read English. He wowed his friends by reading to them in French. As soon as the children were settled, I made mini-trips to meet Art for weekends, out to California, back to Warren, out to Las Vegas, back to Warren, out to Dallas, back to Warren. At times I felt like a yo-yo.

Art went alone to Washington, D.C., and when he told me about President Kennedy and the excitement in the capital, his eyes glowed. "Everything's jumping there, the city is alive again," he said. It seemed in those days as if the whole country had rediscovered youth and love. It was a country brimming with excitement. In February I remember sitting up all night to watch John Glenn orbit the earth.

During our final week in the States, Art and I were offered the use of a condominium apartment in Palm Beach, a chance to rest up before returning to Paris. On the flight back, I sat sleepless and depressed in one of the front seats of the plane. All three children had finally worn themselves out and had dozed off. For the first time, I dreaded returning to our apartment on the rue de Monceau. Kay's recent letters had been filled with arguments between her and our maid Danielle, plus problems with our erratic furnace. We would be landing in Paris at 8:00 A.M. and as I looked out the window I saw black clouds and driving sleet. There would be very little if any food in the house, and I prayed that our hot water heater still functioned.

Just then, I looked up to see Art, who had spent most of the night playing cards, bending over my chair. "I have an idea I want you to just think about," he said. "It's not for now, but what would you think about moving back to the States for a year? We could rent a house in Washington—that's where I'd like to be—and leave everything in Paris as it is. We'd come back whenever we want."

ART: **I guess the decision to go home was in the back of my mind for some time. I had literally exhausted all the humor about tourists, the French, the Italians, the Swiss and the International Set. I knew I had it made in Europe but I felt I was repeating myself over & over again.**

When I went home for the lecture tour I realized if I wanted to write satire I had to do it about my own country. I also believe that like most Americans (there

are a few exceptions) you eventually want to be part of something. Although we had a marvelous life in Paris, we never considered ourselves anything more than temporary squatters.

The other element that made me make up my mind was Kennedy's Washington. It was a mad crazy place filled with excitement and opportunity which everyone wanted to read about. I'm not sure I would have come back had Johnson been in the White House or even Gerry Ford.

But having made the decision I was warned by almost everyone I would fall on my face. I was a "big fish in a small pond" in Europe, but I was told Washington was full of sharks and I would be throwing away everything I had built over the fourteen years.

Ann was very clever about my move and said "Announce you're only going back for two years. Then if you fail you can always return to Paris without your tail between your legs."

The *Tribune* thought it was a good idea. Also John Crosby, a columnist on the *Herald Tribune* whom I liked and respected—we shared the same space on alternate days in the New York *Herald Tribune*—was very unhappy in New York and thought he could use two years in Europe. So we announced we were exchanging jobs.

The announcement came at the very moment that President Kennedy, in anger, had canceled his subscription to the New York *Herald Tribune* in a rare public display of pique.

Drew Pearson and several other pundits interpreted my move as the *Trib*'s way of getting back at Kennedy. They wrote I was being brought to Washington by the *Trib* to get even with the President. It sounded like a much better reason than the one I was prepared to give, so I never denied it.

The unexpected publicity helped me get a lot of newspaper clients that had never heard of me.

As for the family, I knew we'd all be in for a culture shock. Our standard of living in Paris was hard to give up. It was much more difficult for Ann and the children to adjust to the United States than it was for me. But we did it and we're glad. People ask me to this day if I miss Paris, and I always reply, "Only when I eat."

The decision made, I became schizophrenic. Common sense told me that we might not be leaving for a year, but emotionally I was beginning to say goodbye to everything around me—I let things go in the apartment. I stopped buying flowers for the big vase on the piano. A chair leg broke and instead of gluing it back on, I propped the leg under the chair and hid it in a dark corner of the dining room. I began buying staple foods in such small quantities they lasted only a day or two. Neither Art nor I talked about where we might take the children for summer vacation. A connecting link had been broken.

By the end of the summer we were gone. We used June and July to pack household goods, pictures, books, and what I call trimmings. We left a fully furnished apartment behind, including a new rug in our dining room. We would be back, we told ourselves.

We sailed August 30 on the *Queen Mary*, bringing Kay Walsh with us in hopes that she would find in America what we had found in France: a fuller, brighter life and hopefully a husband. She had told me several times, "I'd like to go to America and marry a man like Mr. Buchwald who'll give me pretty presents." Crosby and Tish Noyes of the Washington *Star* brought a champagne and caviar picnic to the railroad station and we ate it sitting on the steps of the Le Havre train.

Three weeks before we left Paris, Art had flown to Washington alone to look for a house we could rent. He called me after a few days to say, "Everything's too expensive here! I found a house with the right number of bedrooms but the rent is $750 a month and the stairs are all broken." Ben Bradlee and Doc Dalinsky of the Georgetown Pharmacy were his advisers. They told him to buy a house which we could sell or rent whenever we returned to France. A few days later Art called again, "I just bought us a house!"

"What does it look like?" I shouted back.

"You'll love it—it's got a hammock!" he said and hung up.

I wrote to Dorothy and David Schoenbrun who had preceded us to Washington by a year, for advice. "We're on Cleveland Avenue, in Cleveland Park, do you know where that is? I have a map of Washington but can't understand it." Dorothy wrote back, "It's in the Northwest. Just remember, Ann, everybody you will know will be in the Northwest." Then I asked her for the name of her grocery store. Magruder's, she wrote back. I opened a charge account by mail and sent them a grocery list two pages long; everything to be delivered at a certain hour the day we were to arrive. We disembarked from the *Queen Mary*, drove to D. C., and had dinner on the table within an hour.

Our children adjusted immediately to the United States. Television, *Captain Kangaroo*, bicycles, open lawns to run on, schools where the teachers smiled and admired, neighbors you could visit by running across a driveway. Only their lack of written English bothered them, but even that was taken care of within a year; one special tutor singlehandedly turned Joel into the best reader in our family.

But it wasn't to be a smooth transition for the adults. Kay Walsh cried daily, "Where are the cafés? How can I make friends? I know no one." Art and I tried to be cheerful, but had our own problems. Art had to start from scratch in a city bulging with competitive correspondents. He was haunted by the warnings his pals had offered in Paris: "You've got it made here, Art. If you go the States you'll get massacred." He didn't mention his worries, because he knew I was as shaky as he was. The city seemed cold and scattered. I didn't drive and had to keep taxis waiting outside of Giant and Safeway. If I forgot an item it was a big deal. There was no privacy, no concierge to warn me of visitors when I was preparing dinner for the children with curlers in my hair.

The house we'd bought was a tall, narrow one with little stacked-up rooms, none big enough to stretch out in. Kay and the two girls had bedrooms on the third floor; Joel's room was on the second floor next to Art's and mine. There was a constant Keystone Kop running up and down four flights of stairs from early morning till midnight. I nearly broke the bank redecorating the house, redoing the patio, resodding the lawn, nonchalantly signing for a new roof when the old one leaked—all well spent, I figured, since we would soon be returning to France and any improvement would mean a higher rent.

At the end of eighteen months as we were getting dressed to go out one night, Art said, "If we're not going back to Paris in the very near future, let's look for a house with at least one more room—everytime I start to undress, someone walks in looking for something."

We called Gertie d'Amercourt, the agent who had found us the Cleveland Avenue house, and said, "If you ever run across a house with just a bit more space, let us know. No hurry, just keep us in mind."

Four days later Gertie showed us a new house just being built in Wesley Heights. The house, which looked like a Normandy country home, stood in a sea of February mud surrounded by trucks, tractors, and building equipment. Art and I walked gingerly over unfinished floors, up stairs without railings, and Art said, "It's beautiful, isn't it? Let's take it."

"Don't you think we should look at least at two or three other houses if we're going to buy an acre of land and a house with a thirty-year mortgage?"

Art said, "Sure, if you insist. Gertie, let's go look at a few other houses."

An hour and three houses later, Art turned to me in the car and asked, "Satisfied?"

We moved in the next month and have been here ever since. At a party in New York years ago, the entertainment of the evening was a fortune teller. We all lined up on the stairs waiting our turn. I remember the woman looking at the palm of my hand, shuffling a few cards, then saying, "Your future lies by the side of the road, and you will live in a large white house surrounded by trees and flowers." She didn't add: "And you'll take Paris with you wherever you go."

ART: **This will be my last interruption. I've read the pages Ann has written with interest. We made a deal when she started that I wouldn't read anything she wrote, and she wouldn't read anything I inserted until the book was in galleys.**

My conclusion is that like most people who spent so much time in Paris, we have tended to romanticize our lives and remember the good things, blotting out the bad ones.

I fear that people will think that it was nothing but wine and foie gras. It obviously wasn't. As with all married couples we had bitter fights, threatened to leave each other, and had harsh words which would have been better left unsaid. But we survived it. In my case I believe it was because Ann knew from the beginning that she had to compete with my job for my affections. She didn't like it—still doesn't—but was wise enough to understand it.

Many of her friends have criticized her for catering to my whims. Most of them have been married two and three times. We're still together, so we must be doing something right.

Paris is very much part of both our lives. Our dearest friends are those we first knew in Paris. The city will always be a part of us. The European edition of the *Herald Tribune* is the only paper I truly love.

Hemingway had his moveable feast and so did we.

Ann Buchwald

Every once in a while I think about Paris. I hope at this very moment that some young American boy is standing out on a balcony in a top hat knocking on his girl's window and asking her if he can come in. And I hope she lets him in and finally blackmails him into marrying her by saying if he doesn't she'll go home. And if that poor chap is reading this I can tell him from experience after you get over upchucking, it isn't a bad life at all.